The
Pocket Pensions
Guide

The
Pocket Pensions
Guide

Robin Ellison

PRENTICE HALL
EUROPE

LONDON • NEW YORK • TORONTO • SYDNEY • TOKYO • SINGAPORE
MADRID • MEXICO CITY • MUNICH • PARIS

First published 1999 by
Prentice Hall Europe
Campus 400, Maylands Avenue
Hemel Hempstead
Hertfordshire, HP2 7EZ
A division of
Simon & Schuster International Group

Designed and typeset in 10/12pt Sabon
by The Ascenders Partnership, Basingstoke

Printed and bound in Great Britain by
Biddles Ltd, Guildford and King's Lynn

Library of Congress Cataloging-in-Publication Data

Available from the publisher

British Library Cataloguing in Publication Data

A catalogue record for this book is available from
the British Library

ISBN 0–13–649054–9

1 2 3 4 5   03 02 01 00 99

Grateful acknowledgement is made for permission to reproduce
material in this book previously published elsewhere. Every effort
has been made to trace the correct copyright holders, but if any
have been inadvertently overlooked the publisher will be pleased
to make the necessary arrangement at the first opportunity.

Contents

Section A: Introduction

Section B: State Benefits

Section C: Personal Pensions

Section D: Company Schemes

Section E: Higher Earners

Section F: General

Section G: Appendices

Preface

This book is written for anyone who has been bemused by the vast complexity of pensions. Even the experts are now confused by the miasma of pensions; but as the state pension diminishes in importance, the need to make private provision has never been greater.

This book is based on the work and thoughts of many others; in particular, thanks are due to Nicola Bumpus and Harold Lewis, my colleagues in Eversheds, Vera Ellison, Alison Mitchell of BBC's *MoneyBox*, who have contributed to improvements to the text, and to Bryn Davies, the actuary, of Union Pension Services who put many of the numbers together. Errors and ommissions are mine alone.

Inevitably much of the information is bound to become out of date, sooner rather than later, since the government is pledged to redesign the pensions system, like many governments before it. Pensions arrangements seem to have a lifespan of only ten years, despite the need for long-term planning. None the less, that is no excuse for the rest of us to avoid the issue and hopefully this book will help you.

SECTION

A

Introduction

Someone else said, 'Any more trouble from that brother of yours and we'll be burning him at the stake next year.'

The laughter that greeted this suggestion was disturbing to me. I looked across the open space. In the lurid light of the bonfire I saw Kristina lift her hand and give me a faint, despairing wave, an appeal as much as a greeting.

I waved back, a trifle self-consciously. I did not move to join them immediately. My attention was distracted by Mrs Evans, a retired civil servant, who wanted some advice about her pension rights. She had been speaking at some length, almost tediously, when all at once she brought her remarks to an abrupt close and hurried off.

Robert McCrum, *Suspicion*, PICADOR, 1996, p. 214

1 How to use this book

An ant spent all the summer running about the fields and collecting grains of wheat and barley to store for the winter. A beetle which saw it expressed amazement at its industry in working hard even during the season when other creatures had a holiday and rested from their labours. At the time, the ant held its peace. But later on, when winter set in and the rain washed away the dung, the beetle came famished with hunger and begged the ant for a share of its food. 'You should have worked,' the ant replied, 'when I was hard at work, instead of sneering at me. If you had done so, you would not be short of food now.'

Fables of Aesop, PENGUIN, 1964, p. 141

The layout of the book

This book is intended for you whether you know very little or even nothing about pensions. You could be forgiven for not wanting to spend too much time on the issue. Pensions mean thinking about retirement or even death, not always comfortable thoughts. And even if you act responsibly, you might have slightly cynical thoughts about the subject – everyone knows, for example, that pensions have had a lousy press in recent years, for good reason:

- many personal pensions have been sold to people for whom they were unsuitable, and

- company schemes seemed very unsafe after Mr Maxwell used their assets fraudulently in the early 1990s.

And even if you are keen on pensions, it is not easy to find out just what you should do. Salesmen seem obsessed with jargon, the Inland Revenue seem to impose rules of Byzantine complexity, and the documents you are given to sign seem specifically designed to give you a headache. It is hardly surprising that even if you are interested, you find it hard to find out much about your pension if you have one, or which pension is best for you if you do not. The consumer guides are not always free from technicalities, and those newspaper articles which extensively cover the area can only give a brief overview.

But there is no need to despair. Your pension is possibly the most important thing you own, perhaps more valuable than your house, for example. Of course, if you do not understand what you have, that is a shame; it also makes it difficult to plan for your old age, because you may not understand how much your pensions will provide, or what opportunities are available to you to improve your pension. If you are younger when you read this, this may not seem so important, although useful opportunities will still be missed.

If you are older, you will already be uncomfortably aware that:

- with every day that passes you have less time to save up for your pension,

- medical science is prolonging your life though not necessarily its quality,

- the value of the state pension is diminishing with every generation, and

- your children if you have any are less likely, willing or able to support you in your old age.

Table 1 Not enough babies

In 1960 there were 3.5 workers for every pensioner.
In 2000 there will be only 2 workers for every pensioner.

In 1960 most women had 3 children.
In the 1990s most women have fewer than 2 children.

So there will be *fewer* children looking after *more* pensioners who are living *longer*.

So it is crucial to get your retirement income sorted out. But it is not easy to find unbiased and independent information on how to do it.

- Since the Maxwell episode, when Robert Maxwell abused the company pension scheme of the *Daily Mirror* some years ago, you may feel uncomfortable with joining an employer's scheme.

- Since the press comment about personal pensions, you may feel that finding an independent adviser is all but impossible, especially if they are paid by commission (that is, the more you pay into your pension scheme, the more they earn).

And even if you do begin to make enquiries, you can be blinded by the number of choices and options that are available.

But retirement provision is a pretty simple concept. You save enough while you work, to support yourself when you can no longer work. Aesop wrote about it several thousand years ago in his fable about the ant, and it is the way it has worked for generations. In recent years, it has sadly become a little more complicated.

- Since the turn of the century, people have begun to believe that there is a 'retirement age'; until then, most people expected to work until they were dead or too ill to continue.

- Perhaps because of this, it is now more difficult to find work after a certain age, even if you are ready, willing and able to do so.

- The state encourages you to provide for your own old age; but the way it does it – giving you tax relief when you contribute to your pension, and taxing you when you take it (it's known as *fiscal neutrality*) – is complex, so that it makes planning more difficult.

This guide will help you to

- make a decision about your pension, and

- help you understand what you have got by way of pension.

And while you do not need any technical skills to understand it, there are some sections which are simpler to follow than others. So, you might find it easier to manage if you dip into this book, and look at sections which interest you most, rather than trying to read it from cover to cover like a novel.

The sections of the book

There are seven main sections.

- A: **Introduction** (this section) gives a quick look at how the whole thing works: whether you actually need a pension, what the state offers, and your different needs depending on whether you are employed, self-employed or a high earner; where to go for advice and what to do to complain if you are unhappy with your arrangements.

- B: **State benefits** sets out the rather complicated arrangements under which you get state benefits; there are several varieties, and the rules change if you move overseas or remarry.

- C: **Personal pensions** gives you the basic information about personal pension arrangements, and helps you deal with questions such as commissions, choosing a scheme, changing schemes and what investments to make.

- D: **Company schemes** tells you how to join a scheme, how to leave it, check how your scheme is running, how to become more involved with it if you would like to, and how to read the accounts and reports you are given.

- E: **High earners** is the section if you earn, say, more than £50,000 p.a. to help you explore the special pension limits imposed and maintain your standard of living unabated in retirement.

- F: **General**. There are lots of other things about pensions which affect you whether you are in a company scheme or a personal pension; they include divorce (who gets what), insolvency (can you protect your pension if you go bust?), and corporate governance (what your pension scheme should do to manage the investments it makes).

- G: **Appendices**: useful lists of abbreviations, addresses and associations, further reading and tables of information.

This book aims to help you answer the questions you really need to know the answer to.

- Is the pension I have got or am considering getting the right one for me?

- If not, which is the best one?

You should then have a better idea of what to look for, how to deal with your adviser or employer, what questions to ask them and how to ask those questions.

What's the point of a pension?

If you are well off, you probably do not need a pension. If you enjoy modest means, you almost certainly do, and if you are part of the vast majority somewhere in the middle, survival without a pension in later years could prove painful.

More and more of us need a pension, because more and more of us live longer and work shorter. If we could guarantee that we would die immediately we stopped work, we would not need a pension. A pension is a guarantee against living too long; in some ways it is the opposite of life insurance, which is a guarantee against living not long enough.

Table 2 How long will I live?		
If I retire when I am ...	... then I will spend on average the following years in retirement.	
	Men	Women
55	22.05	26.42
60	18.02	22.12
65	14.41	18.13
70	11.29	14.49
75	8.65	11.24

Source: Government Actuary's Department (Jonquil Lowe, *Pensions: A Way Forward*, 1997)

Because of the way in which we provide for a pension, pensions are sometimes confused with savings, but there are big differences.

- Savings are not like a pension because you can pass them on to others, you can spend them whenever you like, and there are usually tax disincentives. You are charged tax twice on your savings: first, on the earnings out of which you save; and second, on the income that results from the savings.

- Pensions are not like savings because pensions involve a gamble – the money you pay in you may not get back. They stop when you die. They are designed to be tax neutral because you only pay tax once. You cannot leave them to your descendants. And if you die the day after you retire, all that money is usually lost and gone for ever.

Two other points about pensions.

- This book invariably refers to pensions when it actually means 'old age' pensions, i.e. a stream of income which arises once you get to a certain retirement age. There are of course other kinds of pensions, such as disability (sometimes known in the rest of Europe as 'invalidity') pensions, military pensions, which used to be paid after sometimes quite short military service and often without evidence of need or injury, and other forms of pensions.

- 'Pensions' also usually includes other benefits such as survivor's (widow's and widower's), dependant's (partner's and children's) and death-in-service benefits (lump sums paid to your family if you die while working). Many pension schemes also have other benefits, such as a guarantee of five years' pension even if you die soon after retirement, or return of premiums (contributions) in such cases.

Do I need a pension?

For some people, making prior provision for pensions is a waste of time. It is crucial not to waste effort and resources on pension provision if you are likely to die soon after retirement, or if you will never retire, or other people will look after you. You may not need a pension ...

- ... if you are rich (what independent financial advisers call a high net worth individual). If your assets give you an income large enough to live on, and are likely to do so for the foreseeable future, it is unlikely you need a pension. You might want to make use of some of the tax neutrality available to a pension scheme, or you might be involved with a pension because it comes with an employment package, but you might not actually need a pension. Of course, if you think your wealth is at risk, then a pension is a great comfort.

  Almost a third of retired couples have savings of more than £20,000, a statistic which encouraged the government to index-link state pensions to prices, rather than wages, which gives lower pensions. But most of us have very limited savings, certainly not enough to live off. So if you wish to

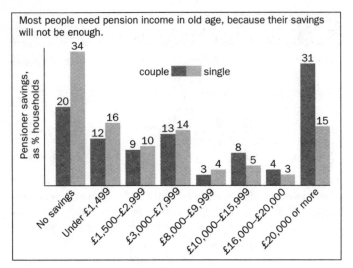

Figure 1 Am I rich enough not to need a pension?

Source: Family Resources Survey, 1995/6, Stationery Office, 1997

avoid Income Support, pensions are crucial. Even £20,000 might give you an income of only £1,000 a year.

- ... If you have a very modest income, having a pension might come as a relief and comfort – but you might find it more efficient to make other savings arrangements. The problem with a pension is that it sometimes only makes sense to contribute if you are paying tax. In addition, the money in a pension scheme can normally be used only to pay certain benefits, so you cannot use it for other reasons, such as to pay off debts or to provide for other emergencies. If your income is very low (say, below £10,000 p.a.) you might find it better to use other savings methods, such as ISAs (Individual Savings Accounts) which allow you to use the money at any time, although you should almost always join your employer-backed pension plan if there is one. It usually costs you very little and is outstanding value for money. But if you can only afford to make contributions to your own personal pension plan of a few pounds a month, the administration charges can be very heavy, and you might be better off leaving any savings you can afford in a building society account.

Table 3 **What are the chances of my getting a state benefit?**

RETIREMENT PENSIONS (September 1994)

Men	**3.57m**
Women	***6.54m**
Total	**10.11m**

*Of the 6.54m, 2.56m have pensions based on their own insurance, and 3.98m on their late husband's insurance.

But ...

While 3.1m (out of 3.57m) received 100% of the full pension, only 1.7 m (out of 6.54m) of women received 100% of the full pension.

And ...

The number of men over 65 receiving invalidity benefit was	**235,000**

but ...

The number of women over 60 receiving invalidity pension was	**66,000**

CONTRIBUTIONS

People who contributed to the state scheme ...

Men	**13,572,000**	
Women	**10,164,000**	
Total	**23,736,000**	(1992/3 tax year)

People who were below the lower earnings limit and not contributing to (or receiving full benefits from) the contributory system ...

Men	**1,830,000**	
Women	**434,000**	
Total	**2,264,700**	(Spring 1995)

Source: Luckhaus & Moffat, *Serving the Market and People's Needs*, 1997

- ... If you have no income at all, you will normally not be allowed to make a contribution to a pension scheme. For reasons which are not clear, the Inland Revenue does not allow people with no taxable income from employment to contribute to or be a member of a pension plan. This rule

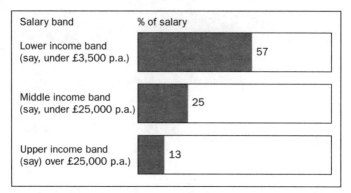

Figure 2   Can I live on the state pension?

Source: Eurostat/Consumers' Association

is particularly unhelpful to women who are divorced, say, or temporarily away from the workforce while bringing up children. They are prevented from adding to their pension while not earning. It may be that this rule will be removed soon, but don't hold your breath.

But there are relatively few such people; the rest of us need pensions. And we need them sometimes not for ourselves alone, but for others we are responsible for. Children, dependants, partners, spouses and others may need support when we are gone. While in real life such support provision is frequently built in to pension arrangements, they are strictly insurance (rather than pension) arrangements, and of course not everyone will need the same kind of cover.

Using non-pension arrangements

If a pension is not for you, there are alternative ways of finding financial security in retirement.

- Personal wealth or savings. The bad news is that savings are rarely as tax-efficient. But the benefits are many:
  - you can get at them easily, which you cannot do with a pension
  - they are simpler to understand and deal with
  - they cost less to administer than a pension.

But although pensions are more tax-efficient (they don't get taxed twice, like savings), it is invariably bad advice to invest for tax advantages only, and this applies in spades in the case of pensions. Don't, therefore, become involved in a pension just for the sake of a little (or even a lot) of tax relief.

- ISAs may be an efficient way of investing in the stock market. Their details, and the rules applying to their predecessors, PEPs and TESSAs are set out on page 229.

Of course, if you are in a company pension scheme, the question does not arise; such schemes are almost always attractive, since the management costs are paid for by the employer, the contributions are (mostly) paid by the employer and any contributions you make on top are extremely good value for money.

But if pensions are not for you, do not read any further; either put the book back on the bookshop's shelf, or give it to a friend who has greater need than you. But if you are in the vast majority of people who very much need a pension to protect them in their old age, read on.

2 The pension system in Britain

One of the reasons for the need for this book is the high complexity of the pension system in Britain. There are at least two kinds of state pension, there are innumerable kinds of personal pension, and about fourteen kinds of company pension. The main reason for the complexity is the lack of any consistent government policy on pensions; as a consequence the tax rules have built up over the years on an *ad hoc* basis, and they are now very difficult to follow. In addition, the overkill on consumer protection has led to reduced coverage. Pension schemes are now so over-regulated that you are now both offered fewer choices because of the expense of regulatory compliance as well as confused by the range of choices you can consider.

It is useful to outline the main choices in principle, before looking at them in detail. They are broadly:

- state, whether basic or additional

- personal, where you make your own provision, or

- company (also known as occupational) schemes.

Each of them is set out in general terms below; later sections deal with each of them in detail.

State pensions

State pensions have a long history; they were introduced in the United Kingdom in 1908 by Lloyd George as an attack on poverty. Most poor people at that time were poor because they could not work, and the reason they could not work was simply infirmity through old age. A simple basic pension of 25p a week was then enough for most of them to survive with the basic necessities.

Over the years, the basic concept was modified, until in the 1970s it was thought that a state pension should replicate a person's income in work, and in some cases exceed it. This ambition has now been savagely cut back, so that state pensions once again are seen as merely a fall-back position for the majority of people. You should not now expect, if you are under 40, any meaningful pension from the state when you make it to retirement age. There is likely to be a requirement to provide for your own pensions privately, setting aside perhaps 10 per cent of your income to cope with it; but, apart from that, the state is unlikely to continue to be involved. There will of course continue to be some form of income support for indigent people, but that will apply whatever their age, and will not be targeted at old people specifically.

The reasons for this change are not hard to find.

- First, older people (who were defined under the Lloyd George scheme as over 70) are now much fitter than before and often very much still fit for work.

- Older people who lived past 70 were once a rarity; now nearly one in three people will be retired, and it is much more expensive for the working population to support them. When five workers supported one old person for a few years, it was manageable. When there are only two workers available to support one old person for maybe thirty years, it is too expensive. We are not alone in the UK with this problem; France, Italy and much of Western Europe has a much greater problem because of the higher benefits they promised and the lower birth rates (see Figure 3).

- Older people are much more expensive to maintain than they used to be; they consume vast quantities of new hips, eyes, knees and other bodily parts which are costly for the health services, and which were never available before. In other words, not only are there more of them and not only do they live longer, but they expect to consume much more. In former times, they were happy to suck a little soup through toothless jaws; now, following a rebuild, they insist on playing golf and climbing Mount Kilimanjaro.

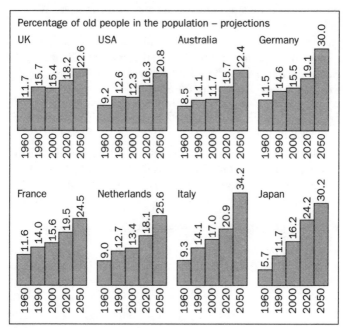

Figure 3 Too many oldies in the rest of the world

Source: OECD

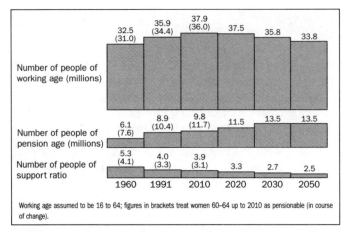

Figure 4   Too many oldies in Britain?

Source: Retirement Income Inquiry

There have been riots in Europe as governments have cut back on pension provision which is no longer affordable. We are unlikely to enjoy such spectacles as we also cut back on our state provisions, since we start from lower expectations, but in due course state pension provision is undoubtedly doomed. But in the meantime, there are four pensions which you might expect to receive from the state:

- the basic state pension (around £65 a week for a single person at present)

- a second state pension (if you are employed, but not if you are self-employed or unemployed) of around a quarter of your earnings up to £25,000 p.a. (around another £100 a week).

- a third pension of 25p a week when you are 80, and

- a fourth pension (which is often only a few pence a week) based on a now defunct state scheme called the graduated scheme.

If these pensions are sufficient to support you, or meet your needs, there is no need to read any of the sections on private provision, with which this book is mostly concerned.

Table 4 What are my chances of getting a non-pension state benefit on retirement?

Severe Disablement Allowance (March 1994)

Men (65+)	7,000
Women (60+)	39,000
Total	46,000

Attendance Allowance (March 1994) (65+)

Men	159,000
Women	427,000
Total	586,000

Disability Living Allowance (February 1995)

Men (65+)	149,000
Women (60+)	259,000
Total	408,000

Invalid Care Allowance (December 1994) (60+)

Men	9,715
Women	13,508
Total	23,223

Income Support (May 1994) (60+)

Men	549,000
Women	1,215,000
Men (65+)	356,000
Total	1,765,000

Source: Luckhaus and Moffat, *Serving the People and People's Needs*, 1997

The end of indexation

The state has long since stopped indexing state pensions to earnings although it still indexes in line with prices (which rise less quickly than earnings). Because earnings rise more than prices, in time this will make the basic state pension diminish in relation to national incomes, from around 20% in the 1970s to around 5% in 2015. Even though it would cost the UK less than some other countries to reintroduce the link with earnings, it would still be expensive.

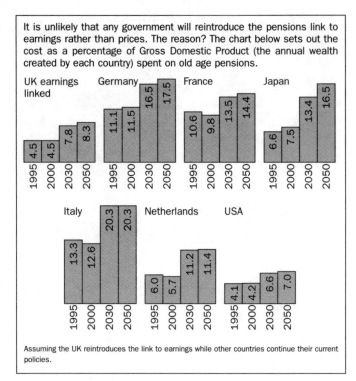

It is unlikely that any government will reintroduce the pensions link to earnings rather than prices. The reason? The chart below sets out the cost as a percentage of Gross Domestic Product (the annual wealth created by each country) spent on old age pensions.

UK earnings linked

1995	2000	2030	2050
4.5	4.5	7.8	8.3

Germany

1995	2000	2030	2050
11.1	11.5	16.5	17.5

France

1995	2000	2030	2050
10.6	9.8	13.5	14.4

Japan

1995	2000	2030	2050
6.6	7.5	13.4	16.5

Italy

1995	2000	2030	2050
13.3	12.6	20.3	20.3

Netherlands

1995	2000	2030	2050
6.0	5.7	11.2	11.4

USA

1995	2000	2030	2050
4.1	4.2	6.6	7.0

Assuming the UK reintroduces the link to earnings while other countries continue their current policies.

Figure 5 Will my state pension start to be linked to earnings instead of prices?

Source: OECD

Personal pensions

Personal pensions have been around in one form or another since 1956 (when they were called retirement annuities). In principle, they're pretty simple. You save enough until retirement, then enter into a gambling contract with an insurance company (called an annuity). You hope to live forever; they hope you will drop dead very soon. Until the date of retirement a personal pension is mostly a savings plan with tax relief. How it performs depends mostly on a combination of expense ratios (how much is spent on administration) and how well the investments perform. You will not know for certain how much you will have to retire on until you actually buy the annuity at retirement age, which is a little uncertain for many people. However if you are self-employed (or there is no company-backed pension scheme), it may be the only choice you have.

Company (occupational) pensions

About half the working population enjoy membership of a company-backed scheme. These also have their imperfections, as a recent report of the Office of Fair Trading showed (although it couldn't think of any solutions!), but for most employees they are a very attractive option.

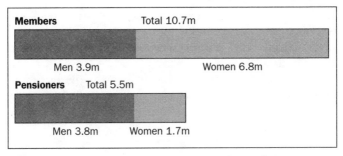

Figure 6 How many people in company schemes?

They are in two main forms.

- 'Money purchase' (somewhat similar to a personal pension) or 'contributions related'. It depends on how much is put in over the years. They also have a risk; they depend largely on how well the investments perform over the years, but the advantage is that the management expenses are much lower, and in any event are paid for by the employer.

- 'Salary-related', 'defined benefit' or 'final-salary' – which are simply a promise by the employer to pay a certain level of pension for each year you work for him. The amount of money in the pension scheme is irrelevant (usually) because it is the employer's problem to see there is enough money around to meet the promise. Because a private employer could go bust (just as you come up to retirement, say), it must set aside money to meet the promise in a special pot which is kept separately from the company.

Funded and unfunded pensions

Some employers, mostly in the public sector, make pension promises not backed by any funds at all. The Civil Service scheme, for example, promises a pension of around a half of salary in exchange for forty years' work for the government. The pension is paid direct by the government, not by any pension fund, because there is no fund to back the promise. There is no need for such a fund, because the government, unlike the private sector, cannot go bankrupt and fail to meet its promise.

Such unfunded pension systems are very large; they apply to the police, firemen, teachers and civil servants. Local authority pensions are funded, as are most other former public sector schemes such as those of the electricity, water, gas and rail industries.

There is often a debate about who owns the money in pension schemes; this is discussed in detail below (see page 126), but the fact that you are in a scheme which has no money should not normally cause you any concern.

Tax rules now make it inefficient to set money aside to back pension promises for income over a certain level (£87,600 in 1998/9); if you earn more than that, you might be given a pension promise which is not backed by a pension fund which kicks in if the employer goes bust.

Tax

Hardly anyone, including those in the Inland Revenue and Treasury, understands how the details of pensions tax work. But the basic principle is actually pretty simple. To get a grip on it, it helps to know first a little of the history of pensions.

In the distant past, there were (apart from the military) no such things as pensions; people simply saved as much as they could during their working life to live on when they became infirm. Two changes conspired to make this difficult for most people.

- First, there are demographic changes to the family (more of us have fewer children, and it is more difficult for most of us to care for our older relatives, because more of us work). It is now less possible for most of us to be responsible financially for our parents. And ...

- Secondly, the fact that most of us, even if on modest incomes, pay income tax, makes it very difficult to save efficiently for old age, especially if there is no 'fiscal neutrality'.

'Fiscal neutrality' is jargon for the principle that when you provide for retirement income, you are not taxed twice. By and large that is the system that applies in the UK (and in most other countries which have developed private pension systems). In the UK the contributions to pension schemes are generally exempt from tax and the investment build-up is exempt, but the eventual benefits pay tax. If there were no neutrality, people would find it all but impossible to save for their old age – and would probably find black-market ways of doing so instead, as a World Bank report showed some years ago.

Pensions and double taxation

Unfortunately, the very fair system we have enjoyed for over 70 years is now under pressure.

- There are very complex tax rules which impose a small amount of double taxation on some schemes.

- Some of the investments, particularly investments in shares on the stock market, are charged tax on their income, which amounts to a form of double taxation as introduced in 1997. This double taxation can be avoided in part by selecting other more tax-effective investments, so it is not as big a nuisance as was first thought, but it does sully the purity of the system.

- Pension schemes do pay tax sometimes:
  - they pay tax when they return surplus funds to an employer,
  - they pay a certain amount of VAT
  - they pay tax on the investment income (dividends) from UK shares, and
  - they pay stamp duty when they buy or sell certain assets.

Apart from these still usually minor charges, however, pension schemes are still a tax efficient, fiscally neutral and a sensible way of providing retirement income, more sensible in most cases than the previous schemes of stuffing gold coins under the bed or relying on the dubious support of children and relatives.

3 How does the state look after me?

Many people, even today, expect to live on the state pension benefits. However, UK state pensions are very low (compared with what other countries pay) and if all you are entitled to is the Basic State Pension, you will need to apply for Income Support as well. And in real terms the Basic State Pension is expected to fall in value. Meanwhile, there are four main pensions available:

- the Basic Pension
- an Additional Pension
- a special extra for the over 80s
- a Graduated Pension from an old state pension scheme.

The Basic State Pension has its origins in the pension introduced in 1908 by Lloyd George. After Lord Beveridge's report during the Second World War it was beefed up, and over the years radically improved so that it now provides around £3,000 p.a. (£64.70 a week) for a single person. This amounts to about 15% of the national average wage, but is still below (marginally) the Income Support level.

It is not of course, on its own, enough to live on; and while at one time it was linked to increases in national average earnings, in recent years the link has been limited to the Retail Price Index. While this maintains its purchasing power, it is falling behind the link to average earnings at quite a rate. While in the mid-1970s it represented about 22% of national average earnings, it nowadays offers around 15% and is destined to fall to around 5%.

	Weekly	Annual
Table 5 What will I get from the state?		
Single person	£64.70	£3,364.40
Wife on husband's contributions	£38.70	£2,012.40
Married couple on husband's contributions	£103.40	£5,376.80
Married couple if both paid full contributions	£129.40	£6,728.80

But it still represents the main source of income for many retired people, and will be significant for a few years yet.

Table 5 assumes a 'full National Insurance record' (see below); if you do not have a full National Insurance record, you will get a lower Basic State Pension. For the moment it is index-linked to retail prices (although not to national average earnings).

The government is now conducting a review of state pensions and the possibility of further privatisation. It wishes (as did the previous administration) to get out of the business of retirement provision altogether if it can. The review is expected shortly (maybe even by the time this book is published) and it is likely to suggest that the Basic State Pension remains (although continuing to diminish in value) but that all individuals (either personally or through a company scheme) must pay, say, 10% of their income to some form of private pension arrangements. It is likely to be phased in over some time, so there is no need to worry about a 10% hit to your income just yet; but it is unlikely that National Insurance contributions will be reduced to take account of it, so that it may look rather like another tax.

The full details of the state scheme are set out in Section B.

4 If I am self-employed

Planning for the self-employed is relatively straightforward. At retirement age, you will get:

- (if you have paid your full NI contributions) a basic state pension

- income from savings, if you have made any

- income and support from generous children (unlikely), and maybe

- a private pension.

You will not get:

- the second state pension (SERPS)

- a pension from an occupational scheme – because you are not employed

- a salary-linked pension, since only occupational schemes can provide such pensions.

You will have to pay tax on most of the income just as you would have done if you were employed.

If you spent some time employed and some time self-employed, you need to work out separately for each period what your rights are. If you're thinking it's a bit complicated, you'd be right.

Who shall I buy it from?

You can buy a pension only from a 'provider'. Only certain institutions can provide personal pensions, which are the only kind of pensions a self-employed person can have. These are:

- an insurance company (in general, any one registered in the European Union)

- a bank

- a building society

- a friendly society

- a unit trust manager.

In practice almost all pensions are even today provided by insurance companies which, despite all their faults, remain the most experienced and skilled providers. The distribution systems and marketing skills of banks and others have still not been able to match those of insurance companies.

There are, of course, several types of insurance companies, including the currently fashionable direct selling insurers (via the telephone). Many of them have long and distinguished track records; others are newer, but have installed modern systems and contracts.

But all, whether fairly or not, have somewhat blemished reputations, whether for inadequate administration, poor performance of the underlying investments, or unprofessional selling techniques.

When choosing a provider, therefore, it is helpful to choose one (or more than one) which has now, and will have until you die,

- outstanding administration

- first-class investment management, and

- sensible and unpressurised selling support.

Such a paragon is of course impossible to find even on current form, and predicting over, say, the next fifty years who will be the best is equally impossible. So the apparent science of advisers who are required to analyse the best performers, produce statistics and subscribe to research services is something of a prestigitation; in other words, it is more of an art than a science, and not much of one at that. You might frequently do as well by putting a pin in a list of providers.

When shall I buy it?

Conventional wisdom is to buy as much and as early as you can. Life of course is not like that. But, if you are like most people, you will start and stop several personal pension plans throughout your life, and this will have an adverse effect on your lifestyle.

Table 6   How much will I retire on?

The impact of administration charges, especially when you stop a plan, can be significant. This Consumers' Association table shows the impact on your pension if you made contributions for five years then stopped and let it grow until retirement.

Age group	Average monthly contribution made £	Average value of pension – contributions kept up until retirement £	Annual value of pension – 5 years' contributions made then stopped £
25–34	68	4,696 (6,166)	722 (2,192)
34–44	129	3,886 (5,356)	1,113 (2,583)
45–54	97	2,011 (3,481)	680 (2,150)

Growth rate reduced to 7.5% a year, retirement age 65. Figures in brackets include value of state pension forecast to be 7% of average earnings (£1,470). A 40-year-old retiring at 65 would live on £5,356 a year including state pension – even if he had been maintaining contributions for 25 years.

Source: Consumers' Association, 1997

How much should I buy?

The state limits how much pension you can buy. It says that you can only contribute up to a certain level of your income (currently £87,600) and then only a certain proportion of that depending on your age.

Table 7   How much pension can I buy?

If I am self-employed ...

Unlimited benefits, but contributions limited to 17.5% to 40% depending on age

If I am employed ...

As above in a personal scheme, but up to two-thirds of final salary, indexed to the cost of living

Conventional wisdom suggests that you should buy as much as you can afford, and as soon as you can. Because the earlier you buy it, the power of compound interest works miraculously.

Table 8 The power of compound interest

Year	Accumulated fund at compound rate of interest per annum		
	4%	8%	12%
0	£1,000	£1,000	£1,000
10	£1,480	£2,159	£3,106
20	£2,191	£4,661	£9,646
30	£3,243	£10,063	£29,960
40	£4,801	£21,725	£93,051

In addition, of course, the salesman earns more the more you pay, so it is not easy to tell if you are putting in too much. In real life few of us can afford, with the usual expenses of life, to put in anything like the full amount permitted by the Inland Revenue (it is said that only 1% of the population pay in the maximum), but we may suffer for it. Pensions, like other areas of life, are a discretionary spend; and we all have different priorities and objectives. What is important for one person is less so than for another. Some will spend on holidays, others on saving for retirement income, and who is to say who is the wiser man or woman?

The main problem is that no one knows how much you will need to live on, how the investments will perform over the next, say, thirty years, or how the administration charges will affect the return; or what effect inflation will have, or what annuities will cost when you come to buy them, or whether the insurance company will still be around. These uncertainties make it all a bit of a gamble, like anything else in life, but you can get an idea of the size of the gamble by looking at a few of the following tables:

Table 9 What happens to my pension if interest rates are 5% when I retire instead of 10%

	men	women
Pension with 10% interest assumption	£1,000	£1,000
Pension with 5% interest assumption	£684	£660

Table 10 What happens to my pension if inflation is 3% p.a. or 10% p.a. in retirement

Year after retirement	Purchasing power of pension with inflation rate per annum	
	3%	10%
0	£1,000	£1,000
5	£863	£621
10	£744	£386
15	£642	£239
20	£554	£149
25	£478	£92

So, it is all a bit uncertain. But you can make some calculated assumptions, which while not guaranteed, can give you a feel for the size of the problem and what you can do about it.

Table 11 How much pension will my fund buy me?

Assume 10% pension

Assume you will live 10 years after retirement

If you have saved £100,000 in the kitty, you will have a pension of £10,000 p.a.

So, making the maximum possible contributions (while paying the mortgage and the grocery bills) is probably a good thing.

What can I buy?

The most important thing you can buy, and the point of it all in the first place, is of course a pension for you. But rolled into the system are other things you can buy at the same time, including a pension for a spouse or dependent children, a tax-free lump sum at retirement, a guarantee of some money back if you die before drawing the pension, or the right to draw the pension a little earlier than you'd planned. All of these 'options' come at a price, which you can meet either by paying extra contributions (up to the limits mentioned above) or by reducing the pension expectation.

Table 12 The options

- Spouse's pension
- Waiver of premium
- Dependant's pensions
- Cash commutation

How do they charge?

One of the most vexed questions is working out how your provider charges. Even today, charging arrangements can be very complex; indeed, one of the skills of insurance company executives and their mathematical advisers (actuaries) is to design a system in which you cannot work out the charges.

Over the last twenty years this approach has become very unpopular with the public. Increasingly, consumers demanded to know how much of their money was being deducted by way of charges, and arrangements developed to help them do this.

So, more modern contracts, especially those sold on the telephone, try to make the charges 'transparent', i.e. to make it clear what they are. But, even then, it is not always easy to really work out what they are, and seemingly low charges can conceal hidden costs.

It is sometimes helpful to look at how pension providers make their living and pay their salesmen and intermediaries. They also have to pay their investment managers, to pay for the advertising in newspapers and on television, their head office, their leaflets and brochures, their technical experts to advise on Revenue rules and legal obligations. It is horribly expensive, and made more so because of the (probably unnecessarily complex) tax and social security regulations. And very properly they have to reward their shareholders and make a profit.

The way in which the expenses (and profit) are recovered is by charging. There are usually

- set-up charges and then

- annual management charges as long as the funds are managed.

Of course the set-up charges can be spread (amortised) over

the future years, so it is important to understand how your arrangements deduct their charges.

Sometimes the deal is that you promise to continue the contributions for, say, 25 years or until your expected retirement age. The problem is that if you stop or change the deal, say, halfway through, not only have you got to pay the set-up charges (which you will have to pay again if you start with a new provider) but you have to pay the loss of profit which the provider would have earned if you had continued to pay the contributions until retirement. There is therefore usually a 'surrender penalty' if you stop the contract early, and it can be quite expensive. Switching providers is therefore not normally to be recommended unless there are very good reasons.

More modern pension schemes offer a more flexible and open charging structure (and often lower charges) but all are expensive, and will inevitably have to be so while distribution and selling costs are so high. Even pension arrangements which do not pay commission, or sell only by telephone have to have staff, printing, advertising and other overheads. Nothing is as cheap as a state system; but state systems have their own drawbacks. There is no such thing as a perfect system; what this book tries to do is to help you find the least imperfect – and the right one for your particular needs.

Table 13   How much does my adviser earn?
An independent financial adviser earns
2% of the first year's premiums   ×   the number of years to retirement up to 50%.
If you pay at age 30 a contribution of £100 a month and intend to retire at age 60 he will earn £1200 × 30 = £36000 × 2% = £720. There is usually a 60% bonus, which gives a figure of £432 =£1152 plus 1.5% of future years' contributions, say £18 a year.

How do they invest?

There is a vast variety of ways in which to invest the contributions until they are needed. But, despite the variety of names and titles which the marketing departments of insurance companies like to use, there are usually just three main types.

- Cash: at one extreme is a simple cash fund, rather like a bank or building society account. The advantage of such an account is its simplicity. You can see on any day what it is worth, with added interest building up nicely over the years. There are two drawbacks to such an investment. Inflation: if it returned with any vengeance, it could make a large hole (at present with modest inflation, the interest should just about keep the real value alive); and, more annoyingly, competing investments (such as in the stock market) which could and probably will beat it. But it is 'low risk', i.e. it is unlikely to diminish in nominal value in the short term, and it is the kind of investment to switch into as you approach retirement age, where growth is less important than security and stability.

- Shares (sometimes known as equities or stocks): these are investments in companies whose shares are quoted on the stock market. As the adverts say in relation to similar investments, they can go down as well as up, and if you buy them at the wrong time you will take some time to recover any losses. But historically investments in shares on average have outperformed leaving the money in the bank. You can invest in shares as a generalist or a specialist.

  - There is a wide variety of specialist share investments: you could choose only UK shares, or only Japanese shares. You can also decide to choose only ethical investments, or socially beneficial shares. In all these cases it is not very efficient to buy specific shares direct, because of the costs of buying and selling individual shares, so almost all arrangements buy a variety of shares both to reduce costs and spread the risks. These systems are very similar to unit trusts, but their administration costs are often difficult to manage and supervise. And because they need expensive fund managers to look after them, to keep an eye on whether it is time to sell or buy particular shares, the costs of administration are higher than ...

– 'tracker' or 'indexed' funds, which invest across the entire stock market. This means that a computer can buy and sell the shares, to make sure that the kinds of shares your fund holds reflect the percentage of shares that the market represents. For example, if BT represents 5% of the stock market, 5% of your fund will be in BT shares. The good news is that management charges can be and should be lower; the bad news is that you buy shares that most fund managers would refuse to hold and which, because of the tax system, are inappropriate for a pension fund. For example, shares that pay dividends have to pay tax twice, so it makes sense for pension funds to invest in a different kind of share, sometimes called a convertible, which looks like a share but gives interest rather than a dividend, which pays no tax for pension funds. A tracker fund could not do this; and there is also some evidence that tracker funds are particularly volatile and can create falls (and rises) in the stock market, because they have to keep switching; the computer decides whether to buy and sell regardless of common sense.

• Bonds are an investment offered either by the government (when they are called 'gilts') or by a company which promises to pay your investment back at some time in the future, and meanwhile pays you interest.

What happens if I want to change my provider?

There are of course times when you want to change the provider you have been using, and perhaps transfer the funds you have built up to someone else. Perhaps you are uncomfortable with the service you receive, or you have read that returns elsewhere will be greater.

With some of the modern pension arrangements, moving from provider to provider may be less expensive than before, but there are always costs. In most cases the provider is recovering the set-up costs and the loss of future profits from the money you have contributed, which is why in the early years of arrangements you will find that you have less than you put in, never mind any growth!

This is the difference between:

- a 'fund value', i.e. the amount which shows on your annual statement, and

- the 'surrender value', the often much lower amount that you would be given if you want to transfer it to another provider.

The question you need to ask yourself if you want to move is whether, after paying the costs of the move, you would do better with another provider. Since in most cases such moves can prove expensive, it needs careful thought, especially as a new series of set-up costs often can be incurred.

5 If I am employed

If you are employed, your choices could be rather wider than if you are self-employed. You could have the opportunity to join

- an employer-backed pension scheme (an occupational pension scheme) or, if there is none

- make provision through a personal pension, in which case the preceding section applies.

Occupational pension schemes broadly come in three versions.

- Money-purchase (sometimes known as defined contribution) schemes, which are very similar to personal pensions, but the expenses are paid for by the employer.

- In recent years, employers have favoured 'group personal pensions' which are not strictly employer-sponsored schemes, but involve bulk buying of personal pensions on very favourable terms for you as an employee.

- Salary-related (sometimes known as final-salary or defined benefit) schemes. These provide benefits related to the years of service promised by the employer. These are very popular, and extremely good value for employees, but their growth has been limited in recent years because of increased regulatory costs and changes in fashion, which affect pension schemes as anything else in life.

In almost all cases if you have the choice of joining an occupational or company pension scheme, you should do so:

- the overheads are payable by the employer, rather than you
- you have the right to help elect trustees of the scheme
- there are special consumer protection arrangements which do not apply to the same extent in personal pensions
- there are usually other benefits (as well as pensions) attached to the scheme.

In particular, if you have the opportunity to join a salary-related scheme, you should do so, because in addition

- the level of benefits is guaranteed by the employer (i.e. he takes the risk of the investments not performing as well as expected)
- there is a form of indexation applied to pension benefits
- there are usually other benefits (in addition to pensions) attached to the scheme.

Why I should (almost) always join a company scheme

The benefits of joining a scheme have been set out in the previous section; in some cases, however, joining a company scheme, even with your employer paying all the expenses and making contributions, may be less preferable than making personal provision through a personal pension. If you are going to be moving on to another employer or to another job, the transfer value (if any) offered by a company pension will often be poor value. Usually you will only get a return of your contributions if you leave within two years; while not wonderful, it is better than you normally get from most personal pensions after two years.

Consumer protection

Partly because of the Robert Maxwell episode and partly because of changes in employment patterns, recent years have seen vast improvements in consumer protection in company pension schemes. These include:

Transfers

All scheme members have the right (until one year before retirement) to move their pension rights from an occupational scheme to

- another occupational scheme (if it will have them), or

- to a personal pension, which could be in a variety of forms.

There are minimum values for transfer payments set down by regulation; these values are likely to fall slightly, paradoxically, because of rules designed to improve protection. You are entitled to a statement of your transfer value free of charge at least once a year on request.

Revaluation

One of the major benefits of a salary-related scheme is the dual form of inflation protection it contains:

- First, if you leave the scheme, the rights you have left behind are index-linked (up to 5%) so that you should not, in a low-inflation environment, lose by leaving your pension rights behind when you leave employment.

- Secondly, if you retire, the benefits must be index-linked (again up to 5%). Index-linking can make a major difference to benefit levels: an inflation of 5% a year can mean that benefits fall in real values by 27.5% in 5 years and 62% in 10 years. If you enjoy your pension for 30 years, your pension could be worth only 10% of its original value.

Preservation

Many years ago, if you left your employer, your pension rights could be forfeited, even if you had worked for thirty years. In the 1970s the law changed to protect members, so that, broadly speaking, once you had completed two years' membership of the pension scheme, your rights could no longer be confiscated if you left. This law is called preservation and is a major benefit of salary-related schemes.

INFORMATION

Under rules called the disclosure rules you are entitled to almost all the information about your company pension scheme, including

- a copy of the deed and rules
- a copy of a benefit statement at least once a year
- a copy of the accounts of the scheme
- a copy of the actuarial report on the scheme (usually produced about once every three years)
- a copy of the trustees' report
- a right to participate in the nomination or election of scheme member trustees.

DISPUTES

All schemes must include a system to ensure that if you are in dispute with your scheme, there is a two-stage process to try and ensure you get a fair hearing; and if that fails, then a reference to the Occupational Pensions Advisory Service and if *that* fails, then to the Pensions Ombudsman.

You might also have the right to arbitration, where a form of judge is appointed by agreement by both sides (with the advantage of sometimes lower costs and in all cases more privacy), or mediation which is often more conciliatory, cheaper and faster.

In practice, complaining about the management of your pension scheme is now much easier than before and can cause great grief to trustees and others.

Member trustees

You may be asked to become a trustee of the pension fund; almost all pension funds now have an obligation (if the membership want it) to allow the members to elect up to a third of the trustees from the membership, those known as 'member trustees'. The question is: Do you want to be a trustee? You rarely get paid for it, and the potential liabilities could be significant.

Following the Maxwell episode when around £400m of pensions money disappeared, it was thought that matters would have been better controlled if there had been member trustees. Trustees have a duty to the 'beneficiaries' of the pension scheme, which can include not only the active members (i.e. the employee-members) but also the deferred members (i.e. the members who are no longer employees), pensioners and their dependants – as well as the employer. The employer has an interest in the good management of the fund, because (in salary-related schemes) he is responsible for any deficits, and may have an expectation of enjoying any surpluses.

So, being a trustee might be a very useful thing for you to do. You can articulate the wishes of the membership, although you must remain committed to protecting the interests of all the beneficiaries, not just of your own group. You could achieve a great deal of good. But at the same time you are exposed to potential liabilities.

- You could find yourself personally facing legal claims for poor management of the scheme, for example for not paying the right benefits to people; and

- you could find yourself facing criminal and semi-criminal penalties imposed by the regulator (Occupational Pensions Regulatory Authority) or the courts if you fail to comply with the often quite complicated requirements of the legislation.

Most trustees find it sensible to ensure that they are protected against most of these liabilities, and if you are elected or appointed a trustee of your fund, you should ensure that:

- the documents governing the scheme include a clause providing an 'indemnity' i.e. a promise by the employer that he will pick up the tab for any liabilities; and

- the documents include a clause providing an 'exculpatory clause', which kicks in if the employer cannot meet its indemnity promise (e.g. it has gone bust) and exempts you from all liabilities short of actual fraud; and

- the scheme offers you some form of insurance cover; one of the best is membership of the Occupational Pensions Defence Union which protects you not only where you are still a trustee, but also where you have retired as trustee and the other protective mechanisms no longer apply.

You are also entitled to training, with time off with pay for such training. Training is essential, not so much to understand how pension schemes work (you will rely on the experts, such as actuaries, lawyers, brokers and administrators to carry out most of the technical obligations) but to understand and manage the trustee obligations you have assumed.

Should I contract out?

If you are employed, but decide for whatever reason to start a personal pension, one of the things you need to think about is whether you should 'contract out', i.e. pay privately for your second state pension. For several reasons it is sensible to think twice before agreeing with your provider that you will be responsible for your own second state pension (SERPS). At first glance it looks quite attractive to have the tax relief on your contributions, and it may be possible to make the contributions out-perform the value they would have with the state. But after expenses and after the change in the tax position of pension fund investments in the 1997 Budget, it is probably safer and more sensible to let Caesar look after Caesar and that you look after yourself. Some people say that since the state is pulling out of pension provision (as it is with the basic state pension) and since it accepted contributions and paid negligible benefits in respect of a now discontinued state scheme (the graduated scheme), the state is a bad bet. Which it is.

But the SERPS scheme is good value for money, and it is unlikely that the government will renege on the benefits now available. And the administrative expenses of private arrangements are very much higher. Furthermore, it is not known whether inflation will return (the experts say never, which is when you need to get worried) and whether the state will give a guarantee against it.

6 If I am a high earner

If you are a higher earner, you are both constrained by the legislation and faced with additional opportunities.

Limitations

The Inland Revenue thought that the tax reliefs in pension schemes were so great that unless they were limited in some way higher earners would take excessive advantage of them. In fact the tax reliefs are simply fiscal neutrality, and very rich people do not regard pensions as crucial to their existence; they have other resources. For example, it is unlikely if you had £1m spare, and full tax relief were available, that you would put it into a pension scheme if all it showed you were, say, £60,000 a year pension (if you lived, and where the capital was lost if you died). None the less, the paranoia persists (although it may be successfully treated) and there are (sometimes quite complicated) limits on tax relief. There are, as ever, ways round some of these limits and, if there are the resources, there is relatively little difficulty in making provision above the nominal Revenue limits.

In principle, the tax reliefs are limited.

- If you are self-employed, you cannot pay contributions to an approved scheme in respect of your income over £87,600. However, while contributions are limited, benefits are not, and if the contributions can be made to 'sweat', i.e. produce higher benefits, you can enjoy a higher pension without limit.

- If you are an employee, pension benefits are limited to roughly two-thirds of £87,600 , and contributions that you make are usually restricted to 15% of income.

This may produce too low a pension for you; accordingly, if you are employed, your employer may wish to provide additional pension, outside the main pension scheme. There are two main ways.

- Using an unapproved scheme (i.e. not approved by the Inland Revenue) which is funded, i.e. a pot is set up into which money is paid in. Usually, this money is taxable, so you would have to pay tax on the contributions put in by your employer; but the fund is taxed at a low tax rate (23%) and you will get the benefits (if you take them in cash on retirement) tax free. These are sometimes known as 'FURBS', i.e. Funded Unapproved Retirement Benefits Scheme. Sometimes such schemes are set up for a group of employees or for an individual.

- Using a unfunded scheme, also unapproved by the Inland Revenue. This is a promise by the employer to pay you a top-up pension over the Inland Revenue limits, but the promise is not backed up by any fund. The good news is that it is quite tax efficient. The bad news is that if the employer goes bust before you have finished getting your pension, you will only get what all the creditors of the employer will get, i.e. not much, usually. This insecurity is a major drawback, but it may be worth suffering in lieu of anything better.

- Insufficient service – if you have fewer than 20 years' service with your employer, you cannot receive the full two-thirds pension, so an unapproved scheme would be useful.

- Tax and contributions – the usual tax benefits are not available, because the scheme is unapproved, and you will have to pay tax on the contributions paid by your employer (unless he grosses it up).

  - If you make your own contributions, you do not get tax relief, but most unapproved schemes do not allow you to make your own contributions (to avoid some other tax laws).

  - Your employer usually gets tax relief on the contributions, but they should not be too large (i.e. unjustifiable as a normal business expense).

  - National Insurance contributions are payable on employers' contributions (from 1999) and on extra salary paid to you to compensate for extra tax due on employers' contributions.

  - Inheritance tax is not payable (normally) on contributions to and benefits from an unapproved scheme.

- Tax and investments – the assets (if any) of an unapproved scheme pay tax on income and gains at the basic rate (23%). The normal capital gains tax rate of 34% which applies to most trusts does not apply to pension trusts, and the trust can use half the annual exemption from capital gains tax (currently £3,150).

- If tax has been paid all along, you can get the benefits as a lump sum tax-free; if you want a pension, you can buy a pension (as a purchased life annuity) with it.

- Overseas – if the investments of the unapproved scheme are invested overseas, they will still have to pay tax on the gains.

- Membership — you can now be a member of both an approved scheme and an unapproved scheme.

You will need special advice when joining these schemes to understand how they work; there are separate sections below on the operation of FURBS and UURBS. Nor are they available generally in the market, although one or two insurance companies now make them available.

SSASs and SIPPs

For higher earners, one of the main problems in recent years has been finding arrangements that are designed for them. If, for example, you had a very large family and you needed to buy ten washing machines rather than the more usual single one, the supplier would normally offer you a discount for bulk. The reason that a single washing machine is more expensive than one-tenth the cost of buying ten is that each sale, regardless of quantity, has to bear the costs of distribution, marketing, advice, management, rent, rates, heat, light and all the paraphernalia of running a business. The same is true of pensions: most pensions products are designed to be sold to lower earners, with modest contributions, high (proportionately) marketing and distribution expenses. This puts a disproportionate overhead on higher earners with higher contributions.

Accordingly, higher earners have been looking for pension arrangements with two main advantages:

- a way of paying overheads and profits by way of fees, rather than commissions and percentages, and

- a way of investing the funds saved in a more efficient manner.

There have been two main arrangements on offer.

- SSASs (small self-administered pension schemes) limited in practice to people who have their own companies, and

- SIPPS (self-invested personal pensions) for anyone, but especially for the self-employed, such as lawyers, accountants, architects and others.

Both of these arrangements offer very good options for many high-earners; they are dealt with in some detail in Section E.

7 Getting advice

Pensions, even with this book, are complicated. Trying to find out what is the best thing to do, whether setting up a pension scheme, whether transferring from one scheme to another, or whether deciding how to retire, is not normally a simple decision.

So, it is not surprising that most of us look to advisers to help guide us through the mechanics. There are several available in the pensions world, including:

- actuaries, the mathematical advisers that advise on life expectancy. Usually they are overkill unless substantial sums are involved, or in the case of establishing and management of an SSAS. They are independent (unless they work for an insurance company) and you can therefore trust them not to sell you anything, and they do not take commissions. They are on your side. But charges are usually in the region of £70 to £350 an hour, and you might need several hours. So most people use ...

- ... independent financial advisers (IFAs). IFAs are now invariably trained, will not advise on pensions unless they are qualified, and are heavily regulated, some say excessively regulated. In giving advice they are required to take very full details of your situation, whether you want them to or not, and may have to devote several hours to finding the information. They are also obliged to give you the best advice, and write you a letter explaining the background to any advice they give you. You do not have to read the letter; and it does not always explain how much they are making both in the first year and in subsequent years, so you cannot always see how independent their advice really is. But most advisers have had a difficult time in recent years with coping with a pensions selling fiasco in the early 1990s, and are very wary of excessive sales techniques. The problem for you is that the best salesmen do not behave in the stereotypical way that the films portray life insurance salesmen. They can, however, prove good value, and you might find it better to pay them for their time so that you do not feel beholden to buy anything through them. They might charge between £30 and £100 an hour.

- Tied agents are advisers working for one pensions producer only; they are more in the style of the old-fashioned life insurance salesman, and they can of course only offer their own company's products. They are sometimes shy of explaining this up-front, and you should always ask them for their card when they come to call. If the card carries an insurance company name, be aware. But they are also now much better trained than before.

- Some professionals, such as accountants and solicitors, are qualified to advise. It is not usually part of their mainstream work. It is important that they disclose their commission if they receive any, and it may be more sensible to pay them for their advice rather than allow them to enjoy commission.

Most of us are not used to paying for advice in financial services; we expect the cost to be built into the cost of the product we buy. However, a pension can be the most valuable product we ever buy, perhaps more than our house, and it makes sense to pay for independent advice. It is not quite like buying a washing machine or even a car; if it goes wrong, it is too late to get it fixed and certainly much too expensive.

8 Consumer protection

Because of the amounts involved, consumer protection has expanded mightily in recent years. It has been enhanced following two major incidents.

- The personal pensions selling imbroglio in the late 1980s and early 1990s. After the government encouraged people to set up their own personal pension, to avoid future reliance on the state, many personal pensions were sold in inappropriate cases, especially to people who were in company or occupational pension schemes who had otherwise perfectly good pension arrangements in existence. The silver lining is that as a consequence people who sell pension plans now are excessively cautious, so that although inappropriate schemes are still a problem, they are much rarer than before.

- The Maxwell affair in 1991 where some £400m or so was for some time lost from company pension schemes. In the end, even before the new laws were introduced, all members of the schemes received their pensions, but it was a distressing time for some, and it was thought better to introduce improved systems. Again, the silver lining is that regulation is now much tougher (possibly excessively so) and, more importantly, there is a compensation fund to cover the position where money is stolen from a pension fund.

There is therefore no shortage of consumer protection. It differs according to whether you have a personal pension, or are a member of an occupational (company) pension scheme.

Protection if you have a personal pension

If you have a personal pension, there are now strict rules about selling you a pension, advising you on transferring your pension, or advice on how and when to retire.

These rules are enforced (usually) by the Personal Investment Authority, which regulates almost all insurance companies and almost all independent financial advisers. In some cases these are regulated by other bodies, but all of them are about to be merged into one super-regulator in a few months.

These rules insist:

- that you receive the best advice
- that your adviser looks at your particular circumstances before giving advice
- that your adviser is qualified (trained) to give proper advice
- that your adviser submits to regular quality controls.

All these regulations ensure that the quality of the advice you get is immeasurably better than you would have got only a few years ago. That doesn't mean to say, of course, that every adviser is up to speed, and doesn't occasionally think more about his commission than your well-being. He too is only human.

In which case you might like to complain:

- for fun (many people do)
- to recover lost money (many people don't complain who could).

The main reason for complaining would be that you had received inappropriate or wrong advice, or that the people who manage your scheme have not done it properly. In most cases the complaint might be misconceived; on the other hand, it costs nothing to do it, it costs the other side £500 to the regulator to respond and, you never know, you might get something. Often the other side will pay you 'nuisance value' just to go away. In some cases you may have a *bona fide* (genuine) complaint.

Many people already have a genuine claim about the advice they were given to switch into personal pensions when they had the right to join a company scheme. The advisers and insurance companies are responsible for paying you back any losses (either by topping up your pension, or paying to have you transferred back into your company scheme if this is still possible). They have usually delayed in paying you first because the procedures for getting the information to judge whether you have been badly advised has been designed by the regulator to be impossible to complete; and, secondly, because no one is quite sure how much to pay. Most pension schemes are not comfortable about letting members in again who left against their advice, or who may no longer be employed by their sponsoring employer. It may also cost them money and inconvenience.

You can therefore complain:

- to your adviser (if he's still in business)
- to your provider (if he's still in business)
- to the PIA Ombudsman
- to the PIA
- to the courts (if you have a great deal of money, or are part of a group which feels hard done by).

In some cases, since time is going by, it would be sensible to register a complaint with the court, so that they cannot object that you are 'time-barred', i.e. out of time to make a claim. But it is not cheap, and you could lose.

The other problem is deciding whether the offer they have made is good enough. What would be sensible in many cases would be to write to your former company scheme and ask them what it would cost to reinstate you. Compare this with the amount standing to your credit in your personal pension (i.e. the surrender value) and claim the difference. Most providers and advisers will cough up pretty fast. You do not need to prove your claim; they need to prove that they advised you properly and their records are usually not good enough to do this.

If all else fails, there's the Investors Compensation Fund which will provide up to £48,000 in some cases, or the Policyholders Protection Act where the industry will provide almost unlimited sums, although it is not certain whether it applies to pension claims. You should therefore hope that your insurer goes bust (so that you can get more money) rather than being simply incompetent.

So, you are well protected. But you must take an interest in your pension, and there is plenty of money to be claimed

Company	Cases needing review	No. of assessments completed	Cases where redress offered	Cases completed as percentage of cases identified for review (%)
Gan	8,770	145	98	2
Sedgwick	6,323	475	294	5
Colonial	6,445	861	772	7
Windsor Life	8,222	172	162	8
London & Man	7,348	887	745	10
Lincoln National	12,531	556	207	11
Sun Life of Can	25,639	1,356	1,226	11
Britannic	12,834	1,701	890	12
Hogg Robinson	1,073	63	42	12
Pearl	39,550	5,304	3,713	13
Abbey Life	16,534	1,422	966	14
Royal London	9,423	1,417	846	15
United Assur	12,067	1,600	899	16
Allied Dunbar	16,792	1,630	791	17
Prudential	59,875	17,202	16,013	18
CIS	42,193	8,013	1,527	21
Royal & Sun All	15,099	2,746	2,274	21
Guardian	8,326	2,004	1,573	24
Lloyds TSB	47,080	9,420	6,836	28
NatWest	13,420	2,308	1,471	33
Norwich Union	6,836	1,228	732	42
Legal & General	33,386	4,328	3,383	47
Equitable Life	10,854	1,412	606	49
Barclays	16,722	5,107	3,599	57

Table 14 How are they getting on with your pensions review progress? (August 1997)

*= includes cases deemed to be already satisfactory.

Source: HM Treasury

by way of compensation if you pursue it. In the first case you should write to your adviser or provider making a complaint as illustrated in Figure 7; a cheque should come shortly!

```
To my Pension Provider/Independent Financial
Adviser

Dear Mr Smith

You will remember that I bought a personal
pension from you on [date] with your
reference no. [reference number or policy
number].

I understand that it may have been sold to me
on improper advice or without the necessary
research work having been done (I was in my
company scheme which I left in order to take
out the personal pension with you).

I should be grateful if you would advise me
of the compensation payable in this case; I
have discussed the matter with my company
pension scheme who tell me that the cost of
reinstating me would be £XXX.XX, and that the
amount standing to my credit in the personal
pension scheme if I were to transfer it is
£XX.XX. The balance of £XXX.XX is presumably
my loss, and I am happy to take it in cash.
In any event I should be grateful if you
would confirm that you will not rely on any
limitation periods if I were to bring
proceedings to recover this loss.

Yours sincerely
```

Figure 7　Letter of complaint about a personal pension

Protection if you have an occupational scheme

You can overdose on protection in your company pension scheme. After the Maxwell case (which caused the government of the day great embarrassment) it was decided that such a thing could never happen again. It will, of course. No one has ever designed a completely secure system of anything, but next time there will be a compensation fund (already in existence) which will pay up to 90% of claims.

In addition, there are around 3,000 pages of law, much of it relatively new, and made by and under the Pensions Act 1995 to give you additional support.

- First, there are the trustees of the scheme, at least a third of whom in larger schemes (over 100 members) must be (if the members want it) appointed by the members

- There are strict laws on reporting on the provision of information, on calculating the transfer values, on making sure you get a transfer when you ask and on confiscating your pension as a penalty for leaving your employer (a law known as 'preservation' or 'vesting').

- There are advisers appointed by law; there must be an accountant; there must be (in salary-related schemes) an actuary; there must be an external investment manager (except in the largest schemes, or schemes run by an insurance company) and there is usually a lawyer with responsibility to the scheme. All these advisers, and the administrators, must have a written contract with the scheme – and you are entitled to see that contract.

So, there is no shortage of legal protection, even before the introduction of the Pensions Act 1995. But the most useful and protective mechanism of the Act is the introduction of the Pensions Compensation Fund. If money is misappropriated from your pension fund (i.e. stolen, even if it cannot be proved) and the employer cannot make up the deficit (perhaps because he is bust), there is a whip-round amongst all other pension funds, and your pension is guaranteed up to a certain limit. This system makes your pension fund as secure as any other financial asset, and probably more than most; it makes occupational schemes amongst the most secure financial assets available. The Fund does not pay out if the deficit is only due to poor investments or inadequate contributions; so it is in your interests if the loss is due to criminal activity rather than simple mismanagement!

However, it is much less likely than before that there are inadequate funds in your scheme: in final salary schemes there is now a 'Minimum Funding Requirement' (MFR) i.e. a need to ensure there is a minimum amount of money in the fund. It does not guarantee your entire pension, but it will go a long way towards it.

And complaining about your pension is as easy as it has ever been.

- The first port of call is your own scheme; the law says you have the right to complain to a named person (named in your benefits booklet) about any mismanagement of the scheme. If this fails ...

- You have the right to an appeal – to the trustees; and if this fails ...

- You can approach the Occupational Pensions Advisory Service who have advisers throughout the country. Their service is free, and they try to advise whether you have a claim and, if so, to persuade the employer or trustees to meet your claim. If that fails ...

- You can apply to the Pensions Ombudsman, which is a full-time service available without charge. Because of the level of applications, it may take some time for your claim to be heard by the Pensions Ombudsman, but the application is free and could cause significant expense to the fund (so they may settle). He can also fine trustees and employers and managers if he thinks their behaviour is unjustified. And if this fails ...

- You can appeal to the conventional courts, from the High Court all the way through the Court of Appeal to the House of Lords, the European Court of Justice and in some cases the European Court of Human Rights. All this can prove very expensive and time-consuming, not to mention highly unpredictable. Some cases have been successful in the past, but in most cases the risk is too high.

So, complaining is an easy option. However, if your scheme is being wound up (perhaps because the employer has ceased business), the costs of complaining will normally be deducted from the fund, so that the benefits could be reduced even further.

Whistle-blowing

If the actuary or accountant discovers

- any of the nearly two hundred breaches of the Pensions Act, including

- failure to maintain proper minutes of the meeting, or

- failure to maintain paperwork such as the creation of a statement of investment principles or appointment of advisers and fund managers

he must notify such breaches to the Regulator (in a process known as whistle-blowing) or face disciplinary or regulatory proceedings. Fines and penalties for advisers can be significant and worrying for them.

The regulators

There is also no shortage of regulators covering occupational schemes.

- The Occupational Pensions Regulatory Authority has a substantial staff of around 50 people based in Brighton, with ex-police staff and lawyers on board. They can investigate a complaint if you make one and although they can fine employers and trustees, they cannot usually award you any compensation, so the main advantage is to persuade compensation to be paid, to wreak revenge or to make an example. OPRA is a newish organisation and is still finding its feet, but may be useful if there is a serious complaint.

- The Pensions Ombudsman, who has proved himself a supporter of the little man against the larger organisations. Complaints can be made without charge, and even if you lose, there is no penalty.

- The Occupational Pensions Advisory Service operates a free service throughout the UK using local experts to try and resolve any issues. Its expenses are met by the DSS.

- The Pensions Compensation Board is a new outfit, which pays out if the employer cannot meet any losses to the pension fund which affect your pension. There is no experience yet with the Board, established in April 1997.

- The Registry of Pension Schemes keeps track of who operates a pension scheme following take-overs. It is only moderately useful, since it doesn't keep track of your own pension. You have to remember all your previous employers to see who is now operating that pension scheme. Still, it is better than nothing.

9   Conclusion

With the complexity of the system it would not be surprising if you felt confused. The following twelve golden rules may help.

Table 15   Twelve golden rules of pension provision
• Pay full National Insurance contributions wherever possible
• Stay in an occupational scheme wherever possible
• Pay full additional contributions wherever possible
• Start contributing as soon as possible
• If on modest income, consider alternatives to pensions
• If on higher income, consider SIPPs and SSASs
• If in personal pension, pay the maximum the Revenue will permit
• If you can, pay for advice by fees rather than commission
• Index-linked benefits are better than flat rate
• Take the cash on retirement
• Seek independent financial advice
• If joining a personal pension, ask how much is being paid in commission

If your employer sponsors a group personal pension, he may have negotiated a special deal for you. Some of these are very worthwhile.

State Benefits

Dr Francis had invented the mercury crystals to power a rocket ship that he was constructing to fly to the moon with.

After Rotha had put the unfortunate sandal maker, who'd come to the clinic to have a sore looked at but had stayed to the end as a shadow and part of a diabolical plan, on the pile, he returned to the side of his evil master.

'Now what, boss?' Rotha said.

'The mercury crystals,' Dr Abdul Forsythe said. 'Then we're in business.' They both laughed fiendishly. You could tell by the way they laughed that the business they were in did not have retirement benefits. There was no pension for what they were doing.

Richard Brautigan, *Dreaming of Babylon*, HOUGHTON MIFFLIN, 1977, p. 138

This section outlines some of the main features of the state arrangements. Some of it is extremely complicated; but it merely reflects the very complicated rules. A simple outline is set out in Section A and in any event this book is mostly designed to help you plan your *private* arrangements.

10 Introduction

For the time being, state pensions form a large part of most people's retirement planning. State benefits, however, are destined to fall as a proportion of retirement income, and private arrangements are expected to take their place.

Meanwhile, as mentioned earlier, you can expect to get in many cases up to four different pensions from the state:

- a Basic State Pension

- a State Earnings-related Pension if you are employed and earn over a certain amount

- a Graduated Scheme Pension, and

- an extra pension if you are over 80.

You may also be entitled to a pension based on someone else's earnings record, especially if you are a wife.

The following sections look at each of these separate pensions.

11 What pension will I get from the state – the Basic Pension?

Almost everybody who has worked at all in the UK qualifies for a state pension; there are, however, rules.

- You must have reached state retirement age (see RETIREMENT AGES, pages 155 and 226).

- You must claim your pension. Four months before you reach the retirement age, you must send in a claim form (which should have been sent to you automatically). If you do not get a form, ring the local Benefits Agency office (social security office) and complain (politely).

- You must have a record of contributions. At one time contributions were recorded by sticking a stamp on a card; since 1975, if you are an employee, you will have had your contributions collected through the PAYE system automatically. If you are self-employed, you will have paid through direct payments to the Contributions Agency (with some additional money collected by the Inland Revenue).

- You must have paid as a minimum at least either

  – 50 weekly NI stamps in the pre-1975 period, or
  – enough earnings-related NI contributions in any year since 1975 to make it a qualifying year.

- To get the full pension you must have paid (or been credited with) NI contributions for most of your working life; if you are married, divorced or widowed, you may be able to use your husband's or ex-husband's contribution record instead. Your working life is the period which starts in the tax year when you reach 16 and ends with the last full tax year before your state retirement age – 60 for women and 65 (or last full year before death) for men. The normal working life is therefore 49 years for a man (65 – 16) and 44 years for a woman (60 – 16); eventually, as the retirement ages are equalised, it will rise to 49 years for women also.

- Only those years which are 'qualifying years' count towards your pension. You must have paid contributions on sufficient earnings to make a qualifying year.

BEFORE 1975

All the stamps you paid and credits you received are added up and divided by 50 (but you cannot earn more years than your working life).

AFTER 1975

Between 1975 and 1978 a qualifying year is one in which you paid (or were credited with) contributions on earnings of at least 50 times the 'lower earnings limit' (the minimum level of earnings at which you start to pay NI contributions, roughly the level of the Basic State Pension).

Since 1978 a qualifying year is one in which you paid contributions on earnings of at least 52 times the weekly Lower Earnings Limit.

- To receive a full Basic Pension you need enough qualifying years (as above).

Table 16 How many qualifying years do I need for a full Basic State Pension?	
If you have been working for ...	Then to qualify for a full Basic Pension you must have a National Insurance record for ...
41 years or more	Length of working life minus 5 years
31–40 years	Length of working life minus 4 years

If you have fewer years than this, you will get a reduced Basic Pension (the minimum is 25% of the full pension).

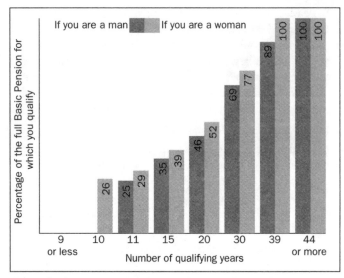

Figure 8   How much less Basic Pension will I get if I don't have
a full working record?

12 What pension will I get from the state –
the Additional Pension?

SERPS

Because the Basic State Pension provided inadequate income,
a second state pension was introduced in the 1970s, now
known as SERPS (the state earnings-related pension scheme).
It was an odd creature even when it was born since it both:

- allowed employers (and later individuals) to elect to provide
  for it instead of the State (in exchange for paying lower
  National Insurance contributions), i.e. an early form of
  privatisation of the welfare state (under a Labour
  Government), and

- provided a state pension linked to earnings, i.e. the more
  you earned, the more you got, in contrast to most state
  benefits which were redistributive in nature.

It provides about a quarter of income up to £25,000 p.a. (i.e. a maximum pension of around £5,000 p.a.), but it is limited to employed persons, and is linked to the number of years' contributions. It was radically cut back in 1986, and again in 1997 because of the increasing strain on the national budget, and it is clear that its long-term future is limited.

How do I get it?

You get this second (Additional) pension if you are an employee (not self-employed) and have paid NI contributions in any tax year since 1978. If you are a widow or widower, you might also get a pension based on your spouse's contributions – and you might get some Additional Pension even if you do not qualify for a Basic Pension.

How much do I get?

The amount you get depends on yet another calculation: 'band earnings'. These are the earnings between the lower and upper earnings limits for each tax year from 1978–79 until the year before you reach pension age (1998: £64 p.w. – £485 p.w.).

These earnings are then:

- revalued each year in line with inflation (using National Average Earnings, rather than Retail Prices Index), and

- added together up to a maximum of 20 years' earnings, and

- divided by 80 for anyone reaching pension age before 6 April 1999.

If you have done the full 20 years, you will get the maximum pension of 25% of the band earnings.

What happens after 1999?

Because the cost of the Additional Pension was going to be much more than the country was prepared to pay (although Lady Barbara Castle disagreed) because it might have required a NI contribution of 24% to pay full benefits, it was radically cut back in 1986 for people who reach pension age from April 1999. First, the deal that gave the best 20 years of revalued earnings was abolished; secondly, the original maximum of 25% is reduced by 0.5% p.a, for each year after 1999 for the next ten years, so that it will only pay 20% in 2009; the 20% then becomes the norm. There is protection for the benefits you have built up from the years 1978 to 1988. The table of what you will get from the state additional pension is set out below.

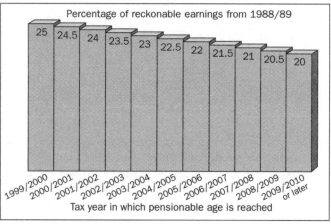

Figure 9   What will I get from my Additional State Pension

HRP (Home Responsibilities Protection) is extended to SERPS when the women's pension age is equalised in 2010; if some of your years in SERPS are covered by HRP, the additional pension is calculated on the basis of average earnings for the non-HRP years.

13 Contracted-in and contracted-out

One of the oddities of the way in which SERPS works is that it is possible for companies and individuals to elect to provide this part of the state pension system privately. The deal is that the employer or an individual agrees to make contributions to a private scheme which will provide the equivalent pension benefit, and the state lets them off some of their National Insurance contributions. If they agree to do this, their scheme arrangements are said to be 'contracted-out', i.e. contracted out of the state scheme.

Whether it is worthwhile doing this of course depends on whether the state lets you have enough to buy the same or better pension from the private sector. The problem is that the rules have changed frequently over the years, so that it is not always easy to tell.

If you are in a company scheme, the decision whether to contract out or not is one for your employer. Even if the scheme is contracted-in, you may contract out by using an appropriate personal pension. If you are not, and you are employed rather than self-employed, it is a decision for you to make, since you can be contracted-out through a personal pension nowadays.

Is it a good thing? Many advisers used to try and suggest it was better value for money. It was certainly better value for money for them since they earned commission on money which was paid into a private arrangement, but none on money that was paid into the state scheme! And it is probably true that in theory you could get better value for your contributions, since it was possible (or even probable) that the income on the contributions would allow the private scheme to pay a pension of more than you would expect from the state. Some of this depends on how old you are and what sex you are.

The trouble is that the expense of managing the state pension is paid for by the state, whereas the expense of managing a private pension is paid for by you; and the expenses of managing a single small pension can more than outweigh the investment benefits.

Table 17   Is it better for me to contract out of the state pension?

You can pay contributions for the second state pension to the state or to a private arrangement. The state pension is index-linked. Contributions to the state scheme do not get tax relief; contributions to a private arrangement do.

Do you believe the contributions you pay to a private arrangement will, **after expenses** and **after inflation** and **after tax relief** give an investment return which would create a fund which could buy a pension which will match or exceed the state benefits?

If there is no clear-cut case for contracting out as an individual, it is probably preferable to pay the full National Insurance contributions; the state pays the administrative overheads, you get an index-linked benefit, and you do not confuse state benefits with private benefits. It is often the case that any gains made by advantageous investment management are eaten up by administration costs, especially if the weekly amounts involved are modest (say, under £25 a week); and it is always possible that the investment improvements will be less than anticipated, perhaps because you have chosen a poor investment manager.

You can find out at any time how much your two state pensions are by sending off a form BP19 to the DSS (Retirement Benefits Forecasting Unit) in Newcastle.

Before April 1997

If your employer's scheme was contracted out before April 1997, you will get from that scheme in respect of membership before April either:

- a guaranteed minimum pension (if the scheme is a final salary one), or

- a protected rights pension (if the scheme is a money-purchase one).

If you were not a member of a contracted-out scheme, you could have contracted out on a personal basis, which would also have given you protected rights.

In respect of the additional pension you have built up before April 1997:

- you will get your pension indexed-linked to the Retail Prices Index (in a joint effort by the state and the employer)

- if you get less from your scheme than you would have had from SERPS, the state will make up the difference, unless you were in a money-purchase contracted-out scheme, when you take your chances on the performance of the funds.

After April 1997

There is no guaranteed minimum pension if your scheme is contracted out in relation to membership after 1997. The whole of the pension is index-linked at up to 5%. What you get is a private pension from the company or personal pension scheme; if from the company scheme, the scheme's actuary can certify in some cases that the kind of benefits you get from the company scheme are broadly equivalent to what you would have got from the state.

There is no guarantee that every individual member of the scheme will get the equivalent exactly at or above the statutory standard. The actuary only has to confirm that fewer than 10% of members would get a pension below the standard; most of course will do considerably better.

Table 18   How much additional pension will I (and my widow) get?

Assume a woman is widowed in June 2004. The tax year before that in which widowhood occurred is 2003/04. Number of tax years between 1978/79 and 2003/04 is 26.

Apart from the figures shown for qualifying level for Basic Pension from 1978/79 to 1995/96, all the other figures are for illustrative purposes only.

Tax year	Earnings based on NI paid £	Less qualifying level for Basic Pension £	Surplus £	Percentage by which surplus is revalued (%)	Total £
1978/79	3,500	910	2,590	341.9	11,445
1979/80	3,900	1,014	2,886	289.7	11,247
1980/81	4,600	1,196	3,404	225.7	11,087
1981/82	5,550	1,404	4,146	173.1	11,323
1982/83	6,200	1,534	4,666	147.9	11,567
1983/84	7,000	1,690	5,310	129.8	12,202
1984/85	7,100	1,768	5,332	112.8	11,341
1985/86	7,400	1,846	5,554	99.6	11,086
1986/87	7,900	1,976	5,924	83.4	10,865
1987/88	8,300	2,028	6,272	70.8	10,713
Total pre 1988					112,876

Table 18 How much additional pension will I (and my widow) get? *(continued)*

Tax year	Earnings based on NI paid £	Less qualifying level for Basic Pension £	Surplus £	Percentage by which surplus is revalued (%)	Total £
1988/89	8,700	2,132	6,568	57.0	10,312
1989/90	9,300	2,236	7,064	42.2	10,045
1990/91	9,600	2,392	7,208	32.5	9,551
1991/92	10,000	2,704	7,296	20.4	8,784
1992/93	10,700	2,808	7,892	13.1	8,926
1993/94	11,100	2,912	8,188	7.7	8,818
1994/95	12,500	2,964	9,536	4.4	9,956
1995/96	12,900	3,016	9,884	4.0	10,279
1996/97	13,500	3,068	10,432	3.9	10,839
1997/98	14,000	3,120	10,880	3.0	11,206
1998/99	14,350	3,172	11,178	2.9	11,502
1999/00	14,960	3,224	11,736	2.0	11,971
2000/01	15,200	3,276	11,924	1.9	12,151
2001/02	15,950	3,360	12,590	1.0	12,716
2002/03	16,260	3,415	12,845	1.1	12,986
2003/04	16,700	3,490	13,210	–	13,210
Total post 1988					173,252

For the tax years 1978/79 to 1987/88 your late husband had total surplus earnings after revaluation of £112,876:

Additional pension pre 1988:

$$25\% \times £112,876 = £1,085.35$$

For the tax years 1988/89 to 2003/04 your late husband has total surplus earnings after revaluation of £173,252. The percentage (see table above) is 22%:

Additional pension post 1988:

$$22.5\% \times £173,252 = £1,499.30$$

Total additional pension pre 88 AP + post 88 AP:

$$£,085.35 + £1,499.30 = £2,584.65$$

Weekly Additional Pension payable to you as widow

$$£2,584.65 \div 52 \div 2 = £24.85$$

Source: DSS

14 If I am a married woman

If you are a married woman (this is a sexist section; the rules do not apply to married men with a working wife), and you have paid full National Insurance contributions throughout your working life, you will normally get a full Basic State Pension when you get to State Pension Age. That age is being delayed over a period (see page 155). But any years when you paid the married woman's reduced-rate contribution do not count towards a pension in your own right.

If you have not paid enough contributions to qualify for a pension in your own right, you will need to rely on your husband's record. You will get a married woman's pension (see Table 18 above) when your husband is 65 – provided he does not decide to defer taking his pension. But if he too has a less than complete National Insurance contributions record, his pension will be less than the full amount – and yours will be reduced proportionately.

If your pension based on your own contributions is less than the married woman's pension, it is made up to that amount. If your own pension is more than that, you cannot get any extra pension based on your husband's contribution.

Whatever state pension you get, it counts as part of your income for income tax purposes.

15 Increases for dependants

Dependant wives

If you are under 60 when your husband draws his pension (at 65 or over), he may be able to claim an increase of the married woman's pension for you. But he will probably not get this if you are receiving another state benefit of that amount or more – or have weekly earnings over £49.15 (1997) after work expenses; an occupational pension counts as earnings. If you are separated from your husband, he can still claim the increase for you, but the earnings limit is the married woman's pension.

Where your husband retired before 16 September 1985 and has been receiving an increase on his pension for you since then, the weekly earnings limit is £45.09 (1997) and the increase is gradually reduced as you earn more.

Once you reach 60, you qualify for a pension in your own right, either on the basis of your own NI record or your husband's.

Dependant husbands

If your wife receives a state pension, she may be able to get an increase for you if she was receiving an addition for you through Incapacity Benefit immediately before she started drawing her pension. But she will not receive any increase if you have earnings over £49.15 (1997) a week or receive a state pension or certain other benefits over the married women's pension level.

In due course the dependency rules will be equalised as the retirement ages are equalised, so that the conditions will be the same for both.

16 If I'm a woman and not working

At one time, if you stayed at home to look after children or a relative you would not have been credited with NI contributions – so you would have a reduced pension. From 1978, however, you are given credits for NI contributions (but not for years before 1978, and not for years – if you are a married woman – which, if you were working, you only paid the reduced NI contributions). You get these credits (known as 'Home Responsibilities Protection' or 'HRP') if (for a whole tax year):

- you are the main recipient of Child Benefit for a child under 16, whether a man or a woman (although if you are a man you must tell the DSS that it is you and not your wife who is the main recipient). Your HRP is automatically granted.

- you get Income Support and do not need to register for Jobseeker's Allowance, because you are looking after someone. Your HRP is automatically granted.

- for at least 35 hours a week you look after someone who receives
  - Attendance Allowance
  - the middle or higher rate of the care component of Disability Living Allowance
  - Constant Attendance Allowance.

For those years up to 5 April 1988 you needed to do this for the full tax year; from 6 April 1988 you only needed to do this for at least 48 weeks a year. If you get Invalid Care Allowance you will automatically get credits for your pension. Your HRP is not automatically granted: if you claim HRP under this heading, you must make a claim.

Even *with* Home Responsibilities Protection you need 20 years' real qualifying service (i.e. not counting the years of HRP) to get a full pension.

National Insurance contributions

There are several varieties of NI contributions, including:

- Class 1, which can be either
  - full, or
  - reduced rate
- Class 2
- Class 3
- Class 4.

CLASS 1

You pay Class 1 contributions if you earn over the Lower Earnings Limit (£62 p.w., £3,224 p.a., 1997). In any week when you earn less than the LEL you do not pay full NI contributions. The problem is that if over the full year you have not paid contributions on earnings of less than 52 times the weekly LEL, that year will not count as a qualifying year for the Basic Pension.

If your earnings are over the LEL, you will pay 2% on the first £62 and then:

- 10% if you are not contracted out of the SERPS pension (see below), or

- 8.4% if you are contracted out of the SERPS pension

up to the Upper Earnings Limit (£465 p.w. or £24,180 p.a. in 1997).

Your employer will also have paid NI contributions, which vary according to your earnings and whether you are:

- in a contracted-in scheme (or not in a scheme at all)

- in a contracted-out money-purchase scheme, or

- in a contracted-out final-salary scheme

Reduced rate contributions

Until 1977 married women and widows who worked for an employer and earned more than the Basic State Pension at that time could choose to pay a lower NI contribution (3.85% on all earnings over the Lower Earnings Limit). You cannot do this now (unless you were doing so in 1977 and have not had a break in employment of more than two tax years).

If you were widowed and then remarry, you can continue to pay the reduced rate after remarriage (send form CF383 plus a marriage certificate to the Benefits Agency office). But you cannot once your marriage ends by divorce or annulment, when you must pay full rate from the date of the decree.

In some cases it may be worth agreeing to pay the full rate, especially if you are on very low earnings (say, £80 a week) since you will actually pay *lower* contributions!

You cannot pay Class 3 contributions during a period when you pay the reduced rate contributions – and you cannot get HRP if you pay reduced rate contributions.

Class 2

If you are self-employed, you will not pay Class 1 contributions, but Class 2. These are the same however much (or little) you earn and they count (as above) for the Basic State

Pension, although you are not eligible for the additional (SERPS) pension. If you are a self-employed married woman who pays reduced-rate contributions (when they were available), you pay no Class 2 contributions.

Class 3

If you have missed some contributions for any reason (perhaps you were abroad), you can pay to fill in the gaps, but only for the last six years.

Class 4

If you are self-employed, you also pay 6% of your earnings (between the Lower Earnings Limit and Upper Earnings Limit) through the tax system.

Missing contributions

If you have not paid National Insurance contributions, you can be credited with them if:

- you are registered for Jobseeker's Allowance and seeking work

- you are unable to work because you are sick or disabled

- you receive Disability Working Allowance

- you receive Invalid Care Allowance

- you are a man (and women, as the State Retirement Age begins to be raised) who does not pay NI contributions between 60 and 65 (unless you are self-employed or are overseas for more than half the year).

17 If I've worked overseas

If you work abroad but regard yourself as living here, you should pay full NI contributions; otherwise you will need to pay your host country's social security contributions. Even if you pay the overseas contributions, it may be sensible to pay

NI contributions as well so that you can get UK protection using the Class 3 rules, although you must pay within certain time limits.

Special rules apply if you work within the European Union (you can use contributions to the local social security to count for benefits here).

18 The graduated scheme

You might also be entitled to a miserable extra pension in connection with a now-disbanded government pension scheme. History is riddled with failed government pension schemes, and this was one of the worst. You will get a modest benefit in relation to the number of units you acquired between 1961 and 1975. You normally get, if a man, 8.11p per week for every £7.50 you paid and, if a woman, the same for every £9 you paid. It is unlikely you would get any more than a maximum of £6 a week, and probably very much less. It is in theory index-linked at the same rate as the Basic Pension. You should not claim this pension if your husband is deferring his Basic Pension and earning to add extra years to his pension and to make it worth more.

A somewhat similar arrangement to contracting-out also applied to graduated pensions if you were in an employer's scheme; you can get details from the Pensions Registry.

19 When I get over 80

A small surprise awaits you when you reach 80; the government gives you an extra 25p a week (each, if a husband and wife are both over 80).

More usefully, if you are now over 80 and do not qualify for a state pension, you get an 'Over-80' pension worth £37.35 a week (1997). To get it, you need

- to be living in the UK on the day you reach 80 or the date of the claim if later, and

- to have been in the UK (or another European Union country or Gibraltar) for ten years or more in any 20-year period since you were 60.

20 If I'm divorced

Special rules apply to divorced women, who can claim on their husband's record. The rules are set out in the section on DIVORCE (page 204).

SECTION

C

Personal Pensions

This section discusses some of the main questions about personal pensions in an alphabetical way, looking at benefits, contributions and changing providers. An outline of personal pensions and how they fit into the whole pensions scene is set out in Section A.

21 Advisers

See SALESMEN (page 99)

22 Benefits

The benefits offered by personal pension schemes are wide-ranging, including:

- a pension for you, which every scheme must offer

- a pension for your spouse (optional)

- life cover (optional)

- a pension for your dependants (optional)

- the right to have your money back if you die and didn't start the pension (optional)

- the right to take cash commutation at retirement date (optional).

The level of these benefits depends on the amount you have put in, and this is limited by the Inland Revenue. You can also decide how much of the benefits can be spread around, i.e.

whether you want to take a full pension, or a lower pension plus a spouse's pension. These are sometimes quite difficult decisions, especially after a divorce or death in the family, and need to be kept under continual review. What you need from your personal pension plan will change from time to time.

No other benefits can be offered by approved pension schemes.

Who is a dependant?

The Revenue have relaxed the definition of 'dependant' in recent years, so that you can name anyone who is not only financially dependent but also emotionally dependent; the change in the rules was made so that you could provide for same-sex partners, who were previously excluded.

23 Bust providers

Sometimes, fortunately very rarely, your provider may go out of business. What happens to the pensions you have painfully built up over the years? It is improbable; in practice the authorities make every effort to ensure your contract is transferred over to another provider, fudging the issue, and while you might lose out in lower returns and higher charges, the basic benefits should be maintained.

In the worst case, however, you could lose everything. There are several places to go to recover some (if not all) of all you have lost.

- The Policyholders Protection Act ensures that there is a whip-round amongst the remaining companies to ensure you have cover. There is a debate about whether it would cover pension arrangements.

- The Investors Compensation Fund (run by the Financial Services Authority) will provide funds up to £48,000 of loss.

There is, unfortunately, no guarantee (as in a company scheme) of at least 90% of the benefits if the money is stolen. The worst cases, however, result not from fraud or insolvency, but from poor performance and high overheads, not to mention poor or inadequate administration.

24 Changing providers

One of the most difficult decisions that you have to take from time to time is whether you should change providers, or start another personal pension with another provider.

The advantages are obvious. It is safer to diversify with other providers, to spread the risk of poor performance or poor administration. It may make you feel warmer inside to have a sheaf of policy documents, rather than just a simple policy statement. And it is great to receive the attentions of more than one salesman, or receive shoals of selling documents through the post. It can make you feel wanted.

So, having a variety of policies does offer advantages. But there are also disadvantages. First, there are several sets of set-up costs, each of which has to be paid for out of your contributions. Second, there are two sets of management costs (although these should not be materially greater than if you had one policy). There is extra administration for you to keep track of, additional forms to fill in, additional forms to inform the Inland Revenue, who become deeply concerned if they see a variety of policies, because you might be paying in more than you are allowed.

The next question is whether you should move your arrangements from one provider to another. The one you had originally chosen may have fallen down the charts published in the papers; you may have had a bad experience; they may not deal with your enquiries efficiently and with confidence. Time for a change. And if you don't think so, a new independent financial adviser certainly will. And he will do so for very good and sensible reasons; he receives extra commission or fees for establishing a new pension plan for you. He will not be 'churning', i.e. establishing new schemes just for the fees. But the suspicion will always be there. To understand the pressures on salesmen, see INDEPENDENT

FINANCIAL ADVISERS (page 220) which explains how to deal with your support team.

If you do decide to switch, the big problem is negotiating a transfer or surrender value. A provider will attempt to dissuade you from transferring your money elsewhere by suggesting that it will not be worthwhile. He will do this by deducting so much of his charges (including future charges and profits) that your transfer value is relatively poor. This is often called a 'surrender penalty'.

25 Cash lump sums

When you retire you can take up to a quarter of the kitty as a tax-free lump sum, and use the balance for a pension. (If you have a RETIREMENT ANNUITY CONTRACT (see page 96), rather than a personal pension you can have as cash three times the remaining pension, which in practice works out as slightly more, especially if you retire later rather than earlier.)

You should always take the cash, since if you actually want more pension, you can buy another pension with it (called a Purchased Life Annuity) on which you pay tax only on the income and not the capital.

26 Commutation

See CASH LUMP SUMS above

27 Contributions

One of the major concerns is how much to pay into a scheme. Should you pay the maximum the Inland Revenue allow? The adviser will encourage you to do that. Or should you put in the minimum? Or something in between? How far should you beggar yourself to provide for your old age? There is no proper answer to the question except to remember that there are other things in life apart from pensions, so just use common sense.

One way is to use projections to see how much you will need to live on. It is unhelpful to use too complex a projection system but, curiously enough, most salesmen do use a projection system that indicates how much you will have to live on. This produces a high figure. If they had any sense they would use a conservative projection figure which should encourage you to save more! There's no accounting for salesmanship.

Paying them

Contributions can be paid monthly or annually, or even as and when. Most people who have a regular income will pay by way of deduction, perhaps by direct debit or standing order. Others, who have no idea how much they are earning until the end of the year, will have to decide each year how much to pay. You can of course use the last six years of earnings and pay a great deal (if you have the money) in one year; and it may be sensible to borrow money to pay the contributions to recover the tax, especially if you have not been able to pay in previous years.

Table 19 Extra tax relief for unpaid previous contributions	
Carry back:	A contribution (or part of it) can be carried back to the tax year preceding the year of payment; and if there were no relevant earnings that year, two years
Carry forward	Higher contributions than normally given for the current year, if self-employed, can use up unused reliefs over the last six years

You can also pay next year's contributions this year (again, if you have the money). One of the best ways of paying contributions is to recover the lump sum the year you retire. This planning is simple, but it is important to ensure that the way in which it is paid in is on a single premium basis rather than an annual premium.

Table 20	Ten questions to ask your independent financial adviser

☐ Are you authorised by the PIA and what is your number?

☐ Have you passed the Financial Planning Certificate, and at what level?

☐ Are you independent or are you a tied agent affiliated to one insurance company?

☐ Are you paid by commission or will you take fees?

☐ If you take commission, how much will it be, in money rather than percentages, in the first year?

☐ How much will you earn in future years, each year?

☐ How much are you insured for, if you make a mistake?

☐ Are you on your own or part of a wider network or a large group?

☐ Have you compared details of my company scheme with the alternative pension?

☐ Can you tell me what percentage of my current earnings, in real terms, ignoring inflation, the pension you are selling me will provide?

Recovering contributions

It may be that you have paid in too much by way of pension contributions, way over the Revenue limits. In some cases you will be able to spread forward the payments for tax purposes (see above) anyway. If the money has to be returned, there may be tax to pay, especially if you have had tax deducted on the way.

Transferring contributions

Transfers have already been dealt with; they are strictly controlled, especially between various pension schemes. As mentioned, however, you can also transfer your contributions either to another personal pension scheme, or to an occupational scheme. Is it worth it?

There may be special reasons to transfer to an occupational scheme. But the Revenue strictly controls payments between personal pensions and occupational schemes for a very good reason. They are worried that by using clever timing you could exceed Revenue limits. For example, if you could get a good transfer value from your occupational scheme, you might be able to receive a pension higher than, say, two-thirds of your salary because there are no limits on benefits from a personal pension. There are therefore limits on how much you can transfer.

Timing of contributions

You will sometimes come under great pressure from advisers or others to make contributions by a certain date (usually 5 April) 'otherwise you will lose tax relief'. You should resist such pressure in most cases and not pay until you are ready; it is true that you may lose some tax relief, but it will usually be the tax relief you could have enjoyed six years before, rather than the tax relief for the year just passed. The loss, if any, will often be marginal, and you should ask your adviser to tell you, in terms of pounds lost, rather than opportunity lost, what a delay would cost you. It is almost always better to reflect carefully just what you want to do, rather than be panicked and pressurised into paying to meet some usually spurious deadline which probably does not affect you anyway. Tax should never be the reason for making a contribution, although it obviously makes it more efficient.

28 Costs: how much do I pay?

See also SALESMEN (page 99)

One of the reasons that personal pensions have had a mixed press in recent years is largely because of the overheads involved. Costs are proportionately much higher than with company-backed schemes, and especially because the set-up charges are significant, the effect on investment performance (and the eventual pension) can be material. Costs are often immaterial in company schemes, largely because the company usually pays for them, and because in 'final salary' schemes the costs do not usually affect the benefits. In the worst cases the charges of a personal pension can reduce the eventual fund by up to around 40%.

There are often several charges levied on your contributions.

- Contribution charges, often about 5% of the contributions you pay in.

- Scheme (or plan) fee, usually charged on a monthly basis of, say, £2.50.

- Annual management charge – anywhere between 0.75% and 2% of the value of the fund.

- Reduced initial allocation rates which gives you a £90 credit for a £100 payment. Often these rates only apply during the early years, perhaps the first two years.

- Capital units, which are bought with a percentage of your contributions in the early years. They offer a lower rate of return than other normal units.

Not all providers charge all these costs and in many cases it is difficult to work out exactly what the charges are, especially since they are often designed to be awkward to extricate from in the terms of the contract.

Lower-cost providers (often the direct sellers) usually charge less, although again it is not always clear just what the charges are.

In addition, the charges often only manifest themselves when you decide to move your money to another provider and you need a surrender value, that is, the value when you stop paying contributions. Many providers pay commission to intermediaries, such as independent financial advisers, on different bases depending on the contract that you sign. If you sign an annual contract (like most pension arrangements), the provider may pay up to 2% of your contributions for each year of the contract. If you sign a 25-year contract, the insurer may pay 50% of your contributions in the first two years to the intermediary. It is therefore sensible in appropriate cases to ask your adviser how much commission he is earning. It is also sensible to ask him not in formulaic terms, but in cash terms; if you ask him, he will tell you. While the annual statement from the provider may only disclose the charges mentioned above, the surrender value will only be noticed once you ask for it. So that it can be crucial in some cases to sign only a 'single premium' contract which results in a much smaller commission to your adviser, and a corresponding lower hit on your pension fund.

Table 21 How much does it cost you?

Most expensive ...

After 5 years	£	After 15 years	£	After 25 years	£
Hearts of Oak*	2,676	Skandia	9,849	Skandia	32,940
Mercury	2,134	Albany	8,224	Albany	27,978
Skandia	2,026	Mercury	7,753	Guardian Fcl	25,284
United Friendly*	1,952	J. Rothschild	7,724	J. Rothschild	25,020
Guardian Fcl	1,969	Guardian Fcl	7,572	Ivory & Sime	24,681

Cheapest ...

After 5 years	£	After 15 years	£	After 25 years	£
Virgin	609	Equitable	3,363	AIG	8,936
Equitable	763	AIG	3,835	Equitable	11,478
Flemings	786	Legal & General**	4,145	National Mutual	13,099
Eagle Star**	914	National Mutual	4,400	Norwich Union	13,552
Legal & General**	928	Fleming	4,425	Legal and General**	13,820

Assumptions: Charges when you invest in a £10,000 unit-linked policy assuming growth at 9% p.a. (* = home service division, ** = Direct arm)

Source: 'Money Management', Jonathan Guthrie, *Financial Times*, 4 October 1997

So it is sensible therefore to check:

- that you are signed up for a single premium 'contract' rather than annual or regular premium

- that there are no penalties for early retirement or stopping contributions

- that you can switch into a free-standing additional voluntary contribution scheme (i.e. a company top-up) if you change jobs and join a company pension scheme, without charge

- whether you can use a no-commission scheme, unit trust scheme or investment trust scheme, all of which have lower charges

- how much the charges would reduce the returns by (this will be in a small table in your 'key features' letter that you get from your adviser)

- that your adviser is regulated so that if things go wrong, you can receive compensation from one of the Super-SIB arms or the Law Society.

29   Death benefits: death-in-service benefits

The death benefit from a personal pension is just the same as any other life policy (more properly, death policy). If you die, it pays your beneficiaries (family or anyone else you would like) some money.

It is sensible to make sure that it goes direct to the people you want it to, rather than to your estate and *then* to them. If it goes to your estate first, it will be collected with all your other assets (such as your house) and, if there is enough, the estate will have to pay inheritance tax.

Using the trust

The way in which the money arising on your death is kept out of your estate is to make sure that it goes to trustees first (and not to your personal representatives) and then to those whom you wish to benefit. The policy you take out with the provider will almost certainly have such a provision built into it; it normally says that if you die before you reach retirement age, you can name

- a particular person (a beneficiary) who should get the benefits provided for when you die and

- a class of people as well as or instead of the named person who can also receive benefits as suggested by the trustees or you.

The trustees have to say who are the people that will get the benefits within two years of your death, to avoid liability to inheritance tax.

You yourself can be a trustee, but it is sensible to have another trustee who can make decisions after your death without having to wait for probate so that your personal representatives do not have to make the decisions.

Inheritance tax

The reason that no inheritance tax is normally paid on benefits which arise on death is that the premiums were paid primarily to provide you with a pension and the death benefit (given as a gift to your dependants) is incidental. This approach, however, is limited to regular contributions to your scheme, but not to additional contributions paid from time to time (perhaps to use any unused reliefs); in practice tax is rarely applied.

You cannot assign (i.e. transfer or sell) your rights; however, even 'protected rights' (those which represent the state additional pension) can also be part of the death benefits and put in trust.

For the situation when you put more money into the pot because you know that your life expectancy is limited and you may not live to draw your pension, see RETIREMENT: LATE (page 98).

30 Dependants

If you have dependants, you may want to sacrifice some of your pension to protect them. On the other hand, if you transfer your pension rights from a company scheme to a personal pension and the company scheme had protection for a spouse or dependant, you do not have to use the transfer payment to include spouse's or dependants' pensions; you can use it all for yourself (except that bit of it relating to the SERPS scheme, if any).

31 Disability and illness

If you are ill before retirement, you would of course start to lose income. Whether you have or should have PHI (permanent health cover) is not for this book; but you could have 'waiver of premium' built into your personal pension. This is a deal under which the provider in effect pays your premiums while you are ill.

In fact, it does not do this, because you would have to pay tax on the payments and there would be no tax relief on the contributions. But the way in which it is packaged means:

- the cost is low, about 2 to 6% of the contributions (depending on how old you are and what sex you are)

- the cost is spent year by year, and is an insurance not a pension benefit, so you do not get it back if you die before retirement

- you will get tax relief on it since the Inland Revenue regard it as part of the pension contributions

- it is not normally available if you are over 55 when you start; and it normally stops when you get to 60 or 65

- there is usually a waiting period of, say, three or six months when it does not operate to filter out those who are actually ill before they sign up.

You can also arrange for your pension to be paid from when you become disabled or incapable of working. You have to be permanently unable to work; long-term incapacity is not enough. Usually the rules of the scheme set out the deal and of course each one is different.

32 Fees

See COSTS (page 75)

33 Indexation

If you have a pension with an occupational scheme (whether final salary or money-purchase), your pension, when you get it, must be protected against inflation, at least in respect of your service after April 1997.

It must be increased in line with the Retail Prices Index up to a maximum of 5%; the requirement is known in the trade as Limited Price Indexation (LPI), 'limited' because if inflation exceeds 5%, there is no requirement to index above that level. In recent years inflation has tended to be well below that level, but if the past is anything to go by, it could be too low to provide total protection. Schemes, of course, are free – if they wish and can afford it – to provide over the minimum, and some indeed provide total protection; the most notable being the Civil Service and other public sector schemes (who have to be index-linked under the Pensions Increase Act 1991). The rules apply not only to your pension but to pensions paid to widows, widowers and dependants.

What are not protected are

- unapproved schemes
- personal pension schemes (except for 'protected rights', i.e. those bits of the pension which copy the second state pension)
- additional voluntary contributions
- benefits brought into the scheme using transfer values
- benefits which are not connected with employment (nobody is quite sure what these might be).

If you move your pension rights to another fund, the transfer rights carry the indexation rights with them.

When you retire you can usually 'commute' some of your pension for cash; it is not quite certain whether you can commute only those benefits earned before April 1997 (when you might get less cash) or the whole of the pension.

The date on which the increases have to be calculated are usually to 30 September in each year, and increases are calculated separately for each year, so that if inflation was 6% in Year 1 (but the increase was capped at 5%) and 4% in Year 2, the second year would not need to catch up. Pensions in payment for less than 12 months must be increased proportionately.

There is no requirement to increase pensions in payment if you retire before 55, unless the retirement is on ill-health grounds. 'Ill-health', for indexation to apply, means:

- permanently incapacitated by mental or physical infirmity from engaging in regular full-time employment, or

- retired on account of mental or physical infirmity from the employment giving rise to the pension.

The indexation can stop if you regain your health before the age of 55. But once you are 55, all pensions must be paid at the level at which it would have been if LPI had applied from the start of the payments, so you might get a large increase (but you won't get any back payments).

Your scheme rules are, however, allowed to say that if they have been paying at higher than the requirements, they can offset some or all of these higher payments against future years' inflation increases.

The law does not require benefits which have been built up before 6 April 1997 to be indexed.

34 Investments

The way in which your contributions are invested is (along with the costs of administration) the thing which decides how much pension you will get. In many personal pension plans, the money is invested in a general pot, in others you can decide where it goes. But the complexity of many plans is such that it is difficult to determine just how much you will get to buy an annuity when you get to retirement. So which of the systems is best?

As in so much about pensions, simple is probably better. There are five main kinds of investment available, although they have different and confusing names from different providers:

- with profits
- unit-linked
- index-linked
- indexed or tracker funds.

With profits

For many years a popular way of investing with an insurance company was to invest in a 'with profits' arrangement. The insurance company would invest the money, not telling you how much it was deducting in charges and overheads, but put the money into a variety of investments (although it was mostly in shares, with a heavy amount in government securities) and see what it would bring at the end of the day. All the profit went to the insurance company, but it would decide at its whim how much to add to your pot at different times!

The extras credited were often in two forms: first an annual amount (rather like interest) and then a 'terminal amount', rather like a long-term bonus. The advantage (if there is one) is said to be a smoothing effect. Very good results in one year would be damped down, and reserves created which would be used in bad years to top up performance. The problem is that insurance companies, being the cautious creatures they are, paid always more reserves than were necessary, both to give the opportunity to grant terminal bonuses and to make reserves 'just in case'. It was therefore very difficult to see just how well your fund was doing at any time, and it was largely at the decision of the insurance company's in-house actuary at the time whether you did well or not. Most of the effort went into packaging and presentation, rather than into performance. So, in later years, a much more popular system became available for consumers ...

Unit-linked system

... the unit-linked system. On the surface this looked much more attractive, and rather similar to the increasingly familiar unit trusts. No longer, in theory at least, were you at the mercy of over-cautious insurance company managers who kept back your money to benefit the next generation or perhaps no generation at all, but all the returns (and, of course, the losses) were revealed each year in the fund in which you were invested. Not only that, but in some cases you could choose which fund to invest in, according to your needs and aspirations. You could choose a high-risk fund in the early years, perhaps in smaller companies in the stock market, and then become more cautious in later years, moving your contributions to less volatile investments such as government bonds. It was more difficult for insurance companies to hide their inadequate performance and easier for the consumer magazines to compile performance tables to see how your money was doing, and whether other companies were doing better. For a while, it became highly popular, but insurance companies still needed to remunerate their introducers of business, and it was crucial that hidden expenses were reserved to pay the intermediaries and advisers (and the insurance company itself) in such a way as not to horrify the consumer. The charges were therefore still high, and still hidden, and full transparency was impossible for consumers to find. Furthermore, at times of high inflation, however well the fund performed, it was difficult to ensure that kept pace with inflation. So ...

Index-linked funds

... index-linked funds became available in the late 1970s (as special forms of government bonds also became available). Here the investment offered was a simpler one; all it had to do was beat inflation by a modest amount, say 2% or 3% a year. It did this by investing in special index-linked bonds issued by the government. They were safe, and maintained their real value, but the public by and large sought something rather more exciting, considering the returns that the stock market was offering in the later 1970s and 1980s (a bull market, i.e. a market that was rising and offering spectacular returns). On the other hand, they were keen not to lose either the safety of index-linked returns or the advantages of low charges. So ...

Indexed (tracker) funds

... indexed or tracker funds became available. These are the fashion of the moment and, very simply, work by ensuring that you are invested in the stock market in exactly the same proportion that the stock market is. For example, if BT shares represent, say, 2% of the stock market, your fund has 2% of its money in BT. The good news is that whether the market rises or falls, your funds do exactly the same, less any charges. The advantage is that it is much less expensive to invest this way since no thinking is involved. The investment manager needs a powerful computer to ensure the fund buys and sells shares to match the index, but there is no need for expensive fund managers and their braces and suits to be paid for.

There is nothing perfect, of course, and indexed funds have their own problems. One is that the computer software is self-destructive. If the market collapses, it may collapse because the computers all told the same fund managers to sell at the same time – and that may be just the time to buy! It cannot try to beat the market, because it *is* the market. And the index you have chosen to track may not be the right one. You might

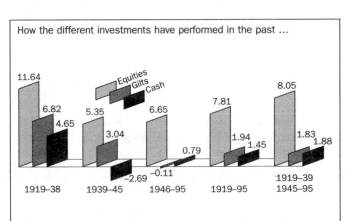

How the different investments have performed in the past ...

Equities / Gilts / Cash

11.64   6.82   4.65   5.35   3.04   6.65   0.79   -2.69   -0.11   7.81   1.94   1.45   8.05   1.83   1.88

1919–38   1939–45   1946–95   1919–95   1919–39 / 1945–95

... but the risks are higher with shares; between 1919 and 1995 volatility (i.e. deviation from the norm) was 4.32 for cash, 13.26 for gilts and 25.51 for shares. Much depends on the time you invest.

Source: BZW, *BZW Equity-Gilt Study*, 1996

Figure 10 Should I invest in the stock market?

want to follow the US index, or Japanese, but usually only the UK is available, and you may also need a mixture of funds for your own circumstances. The jury is still out on tracker funds, but they are yet another opportunity – and it is true that they are cheaper to run. The argument has always been that no fund manager on average can beat the market – which is true, of course, but what you try to do is to select a manager who performs above average.

35 Life cover

You can also use your personal pension scheme to buy life assurance; the advantage of buying through your pension scheme is that you get tax relief on your premiums which you do not get if you buy direct.

You get full tax relief (depending on whether you are employed or self-employed) and you can even use the life policy as security for borrowing money (which you cannot do with your pension).

36 Mis-sold personal pensions

The personal pensions 'fiasco', as it has been called, should by all accounts now be history, but it rumbles on seemingly for ever. By the mid-1980s, major concerns were arising in connection with pensions.

- First, that too many people were still reliant on the state for their pension.

- Secondly, that occupational pension schemes, in which half the working population were members, had significant drawbacks when people changed jobs, and that it was inhibiting mobility of labour.

- Thirdly, that occupational scheme members had no stake in the performance or otherwise of the assets backing their pension promises; they were not, therefore, in a later phrase, 'members of a stakeholders society'.

- Fourthly, that company schemes were too complicated.

The personal pension would solve all these problems.

A well-known industry figure noted at the time that personal pensions were not complicated because they had not been invented yet. Eventually, it was seen that personal pensions had problems of their own; meanwhile, the reforms included:

- allowing people not to be forced to be members of occupational schemes

- inventing personal pensions (which were really a re-invention of the already existing self-employed retirement annuities, but making them available to people who could have joined a company scheme)

- giving a government incentive (which some called a bribe) of 2% of salary up to a certain amount to those who agreed to leave the state scheme and take out a personal pension, and

- encouraging people to take an interest in their own pension and the investments of their assets.

While it did have some impact in creating a greater interest in how wealth was created, and in being part of the great campaign against industrial unrest by giving people a more direct interest in the growth in the value of shares and the well-being of the companies that they represented, with hindsight there were several problems:

- many people did leave company schemes, but replaced their provisions either with nothing, or very modest pensions indeed

- those who decided to leave the second state scheme (SERPS) found in many cases that the costs of administration burned up the value of the contributions they made to insurance companies in place of their contributions to the state

- most people found it very difficult to get truly independent advice on what was best for them in a very complicated situation made worse by misleading government advertising.

This last was somewhat surprising because just at the time that personal pensions were introduced a new law protecting consumers from insurance salesmen was also introduced: the Financial Services Act 1986, which made it an offence to advise on pensions and insurance without being authorised to do so; and those who did advise had to comply with a large book of rules. One of those rules was the 'best advice rule'; another was 'know your customer'. Both these rules meant that any salesman who advised a member of a company scheme had to look very carefully at the terms and conditions of that scheme to make a comparison between that and the personal pension alternative that he could offer. In most cases (though not all) membership of the company scheme would have been preferable, and certainly the comparison could not have been carried out effectively except at a great expense and skill which was not at the command of the salesman.

Backed by government support, the benefit of the bribe, and the fact that the controlling legislation was not yet sufficiently understood by salesmen, over 8 million people were sold personal pensions, many of them being those who should have been advised to stay just where they were. In addition, the cost of the bribe from the government budgeted at £750 million rose to over £10,000 million. One civil servant criticised for the immense increase in cost replied that it was evidence of a great success. 'Any more successes like that,' commented the MP who had been quizzing him in a House of Commons inquiry, 'and we are all ruined.'

What to do

If you were sold a personal pension, or were persuaded to leave a company scheme when you should have stayed in it, you have a number of remedies.

First, you should write (by Recorded Delivery) to the person who sold you the personal pension, complaining and asking whether your case has yet been reviewed as it ought to have been. You should then receive a questionnaire to complete in which you should state (if it is true) that you did not realise that at the time the company scheme was better, and that you would have stayed in it unless you had been persuaded otherwise by the salesman. You should also write to your scheme (or your former scheme), asking what it would cost you to re-join the scheme now and pay for all the years you had not been a member.

If you get no reply from the salesman or insurance company, write to the PIA who have a special unit that takes care of such things; they will then act as the provider or salesman.

Eventually you will get a letter from someone offering either to reinstate you in the company scheme with no loss (which you should normally accept with speed) or to pay you some money in compensation, or to accept extra money paid into your personal pension.

You need to take several factors into account before making a decision.

- Is the offer enough? The amount you will have been offered is one calculated in accordance with unbelievably complex guidelines set down by the regulators but it is unlikely to buy you the lost years of membership. It will therefore meet the requirement of the regulators, but you might (almost certainly would) be offered in most cases considerably more if you went in front of a judge.

- If you want to go before a judge, are you 'in time'? You must normally file proceedings within six years of the time you knew you could make a claim, and you may be out of time. If you bought your pension from a bank, this is not a problem, because the banks have said they will not rely on being out of time as a defence.

- In any event, do you really want to go in front of a judge? It could take years, be very expensive, and you might even lose and have to pay not only your legal costs but those of the insurance company or salesman as well, which would add insult to injury, not to mention the time and worry involved for you.

- Should you take the offer of an increase to your personal pension, the offer that most would like you to accept? It looks okay, but do you really want to have a pension with the company that you no longer have faith in? In addition, the pension would need to be taxed, whereas damages if paid to you direct are paid free of tax, and you do not have to spend the money you receive on a pension.

After having thought about it, make the claim. You cannot lose, and you might gain a substantial amount; most compensation is now at the £15,000 to £20,000 level.

37 Open market option

Specialisation is the key to success in many areas, and pensions are no exception to the general rule. The pension provider you have chosen, or the variety of pension providers you have chosen, may be excellent at administration, or wizard at investment – but they may be less expert in the organisation of annuities. Annuities are the contract you have to buy at a certain age with an insurance company of your choice; you do not have to buy your annuity at retirement age from the pension provider you have been saving with. This gives you the opportunity to get the best annuity at the time; and the differences between one company and another can be quite considerable. This is in contrast, for example, with the situation on the continent, where in most countries insurance companies are not allowed to compete on annuity terms.

It so happens that for internal reasons insurance companies may need at certain times in their year to put annuities on their books or they may not have capacity to offer annuities and therefore offer unattractive rates. The trick therefore is to do a search of the best terms available at the date of retirement and then choose the best company offer at the time; there is no advantage to remaining loyal at that stage to your pension provider.

38 Pension

There is no limit on the amount of pension you can buy, provided there is enough money in the kitty. The limit to your personal pension is the amount you can put in. You can take the pension at any time between 50 and 75, whether you continue working or not. You can also have a series of pensions, taking them at different retirement ages, although you cannot take part of a pension from one plan.

Open market option

This allows you to buy your pension from another provider; see OPEN MARKET OPTION (page 89).

Tax

You have to pay tax on the pension when you get it; this is why it is sensible to take as much of the pot in cash (on which you do not pay tax). The amount that is left must be used to buy a pension (although there are ways to defer that; see INCOME DRAWDOWN, page 167). The pension, whether paid to you, your dependent survivor or other dependant, is subject to earned income tax. The tax is charged under Schedule E (i.e. as though you were employed) whether you are employed or self-employed; in practice this means the pension is paid subject to your full tax (the first few payments will be under emergency coding). (The position of tax on retirement annuities, the old form of personal pension, is slightly different; the basic rate tax (currently 23%) is deducted and any extra tax is paid by you.)

What kind of pension do I want?

The biggest problem is deciding which kind of pension to choose, using what is left in the plan after taking the cash. You could use the money to buy, for example:

- a single life annuity (i.e. a pension that stops on your death), payable
  - (say) annually in arrears, or
  - (say) monthly in advance (which would pay you a bit less)

and in either case

  - (say) for a minimum of five years, so that if you died before the end of five years, you (or rather your estate) would get something for your money. The guarantee would obviously mean you get a slightly lower pension (even lower if the guarantee were for ten years), or

- (say) for a minimum of five years but increasing by 3% p.a. compound, payable quarterly in advance (which would mean you get even less);

● a joint annuity, during your life or of you and your spouse. How much this will reduce the pension will depend on the age of your spouse.

Before you get to retirement age it is worth getting a variety of quotes along these lines to see what the different pensions would be; you can decide in the light of your own circumstances what you actually want or can afford.

Return of fund

If you died before you had the opportunity to draw the pension, you might feel as you gazed down that the pension provider had had a pretty good deal. You can arrange (for a fee) that if you die before taking any benefits, you or your estate will get:

● return of contributions with interest

● return of contributions with interest (say, 3%)

● return of the accumulated fund.

Whatever option you choose will either cost you more (bearing in mind the maximum contributions you can make) or result in reduced benefits.

Life cover

see DEATH BENEFITS! (page 78)

39 Pension providers: which one?

There is no shortage of providers seeking your money: they all seem to offer the best investment returns, the most responsive administration, the most caring approach. Looking at the long-term track record is one way of choosing, reading the financial press is another; using an independent financial adviser, or just liking the salesman who comes to call is the most common. With some notorious exceptions (which unfortunately cannot be named here), whichever you choose will have their pros and cons, and if you have some time to go before retirement, it is impossible to predict who will perform well over the next 10 or 20 or 30 years.

There are two main groups of providers: the insurers and the others.

The others

There are several institutions who are permitted to offer pension plans. They include:

- the banks

- building societies, if there are any left

- friendly societies

- unit trust managers.

Even though they have had the opportunity for many years to come into the market, it is odd that very few of them have managed to make any impression, despite the fact the insurance companies have not always offered the finest service that the consumer could require. Banks and building societies offer deposit-based personal pensions, that is, you deposit your money with them just like a bank or building society account. The money is then simply left on deposit. While this seems to be the safest (the nominal value of the money will not diminish, unlike an investment in shares which could and probably will fall from time to time), historically money left on deposit has not performed as well as investments in shares. And the bank and building societies have not historically been very good at explaining how pensions work, or how their offerings can give advantages; most importantly, their staff do not seem to have the experience or training to explain their products. So they have rather languished, which is probably just as well. Oddly, they do very well in the United States, where you would expect consumers to be better informed.

Insurance companies

Insurance companies are one of the great unloved, along with journalists, estate agents and lawyers. And there are very good reasons for that: they are expensive, not always administratively effective, often arrogant, and frequently poor performers. The problem is that no one yet has devised an alternative that works in most cases. So they continue, often operating like dinosaurs, often employing staff who could not get jobs elsewhere. But they are usually reliable, usually safe and they have a long track record. From time to time they get re-invented or design a new product: there are now several groups of insurance companies.

- The old long-established companies (Legal & General, Norwich Union, the Scottish insurers) who have great experience, but are not always at the forefront of innovation. They will offer the more fashionable products some years after the others, they are slower to move, but they are widely trusted.

- The newer companies (such as the insurance companies linked to banks, for example, NatWest Life, or Allied Dunbar) who are often considered more aggressive, have more determined marketing and better TV ads. They often offer more useful or certainly more modern plans and simpler language, but their overheads are very similar (and sometimes in excess of) the older insurers, and their investment records are mixed.

- The new mail-order companies (Virgin, Marks & Spencer and some of the spin-offs of older companies such as Eagle Star Direct) who suggest that if they cut the cost of salesmen, the savings can be passed on to you. These are often fine, although they often have a limited record, and you have to be able to talk freely on the phone to someone rather than meet them face to face. Since they usually refuse to offer advice, you have to know what you need, and your own situation needs to be simple to be able to fill in the forms. Unlike car insurance, or even banking, pensions are rather more complicated and are not always suited to be dealt with over the phone. In theory they should do very well; in practice they have only picked up a small share of the market. It is still too early to tell whether they will manage to put more than a dent in the conventional way of selling or buying pensions.

A salesman, even an independent financial adviser, will not recommend any of the third group, because they do not offer commission, unless you agree to pay fees.

40 Retirement age

You can, within reason, choose whichever retirement age you wish. However,

- if you retire early, you will draw the pension for longer, and have less time to build up your fund; and

- if you retire later, you will draw the pension for less time, and it will be higher, and you may die before you would feel you have had value for money.

There is no general advice; you will have to decide whether you can afford to retire at certain dates. The Inland Revenue, however, insist that you start drawing your pension by the age of 75 at least, and by that date you must buy an annuity.

You cannot normally start to take your pension until you are 50, although there are special exceptions to this rule for people such as professional footballers, who are considered to wear out early.

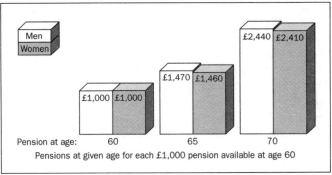

Figure 11 How much your pension will increase if you delay

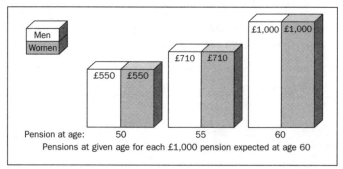

Men
Women

£1,000 £1,000

£710 £710

£550 £550

Pension at age: 50   55   60
Pensions at given age for each £1,000 pension expected at age 60

Figure 12   How much your pension will diminish if you take it early

41   Retirement Annuity Contracts

There was an older kind of personal pension called a
Retirement Annuity Contract (sometimes also known as s.226
after the section of the Income and Corporation Taxes Act
which governed it). If you have one or more of these, it is
sometimes useful to hang on to it because it offers certain
advantages over the newer personal pension. If you don't, do
not bother to read on, because it is too late for you to do
anything about it.

Retirement Annuity Contracts (RACs) ceased to be issued
after personal pensions were introduced in 1988. They are very
similar to personal pensions in many ways, but there are some
significant distinctions.

Contribution limits

Compared with personal pensions, the amounts you can put
in are a little lower (Figure 13). But there is no earnings cap,
so contributions may be made on the whole of your income.
This is the reason that so many contracts which were in
existence at that time have not been switched to personal
pensions. You can switch from a RAC to a personal pensions,
but not the other way round. You can of course have both
types of plan running, but the RAC limits apply if you keep
paying into one.

The drafting of the rules of these schemes often had a great

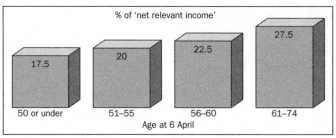

Figure 13 Retirement Annuity Contract limits

deal lacking (old-fashioned rules and impenetrable wording) and it would be sensible, if you have these contracts, to check that they have been amended to offer protection against your bankruptcy and that they are written UNDER TRUST (see page 104) to help with mitigating inheritance tax.

Table 22 Comparison between RACs and personal pensions		
	RAC	Personal pension
Retirement age	60–75	50–75
Tax-free cash	3 times the annuity remaining after cash removed	25% of fund
Carry back/forward	✔	✔
Extra goodies	✔	✔
Contract out of state scheme?	✗	✔
Cash limit?	£150,000 (unless taken out before 17.3.87)	None
Tax relief on contributions at source	✗	Yes for employed only
Can employer contribute?	✗	✔
Receive transfers?	✗ (except from RACs)	✔
Pay transfers?	✔	✔
Write in trust?	✔	✔
Open market option	✔	✔
Income withdrawal	✗	✔

42 Retirement benefits

You can have a variety of benefits on retirement including:

- a PENSION (see page 90)
- a CASH LUMP SUM (see page 72)

43 Retirement: early

You cannot normally start to draw your benefits before the time specified in the personal pension agreement, and in any case not before the age of 50, unless there are special circumstances.

44 Retirement: late

There is no need to take the pension at the age you have planned for in the personal pension, although the Inland Revenue insist that you do start to draw it by the age of 75. You (or your estate) may have to pay some inheritance tax, however, if you die before you start to draw your pension.

Inheritance tax

If you want to, you can retire later than the normal retirement age written into your personal pension. You can, if you want, use 50 or later as the normal age; but you must be careful if you do not take your benefits before death that the money will be considered to be part or your estate on death and therefore subject to inheritance tax. This is because otherwise it looks like you intended to increase the benefits for someone else; if you know you are dying from a terminal illness or are uninsurable and you then put the benefits into trust or pay extra contributions into the fund, you will certainly raise an eyebrow. If you can, you should live for at least two years after you have done this, when the Inland Revenue (Capital Taxes Office) will be much less interested.

45 Salesmen: dealing with salesmen

Advisers and salesmen are now much improved in comparison with previous years. Most are now reasonably well trained, in some cases excessively cautious, and usually invariably polite.

But the old-fashioned foot-in-door brash young salesman is still very much about, driven by commission and a need to meet targets. In fact, however, the most dangerous is the consummate salesman who does not give the impression of selling anything and just seems to be doing you a favour.

Whichever kind you meet, and if you have a pension you are comfortable with, you may need to employ one or two techniques to enable you to get back to watching the telly.

- First, tell him you are in a company pension scheme (even if it is not true). The training is such that few pension providers will accept a premium from anyone who is in a company scheme unless the adviser has filled up several notebooks on arguing why it is a good idea, and head office have also approved the deal; the costs of the pension mis-selling fiasco are burnt too deep in management's eyes.

- Second, mention that you need to have the commission disclosed up-front. You need this in writing, on official notepaper, before you even consent to explore whether you will sign a contract.

- Always sign a policy document at home as it gives you ten days to pull out of the agreement. If you sign in someone's office or their own premises, you do not have the protection of the 'cooling-off period', that is, time to reflect after you have signed up to a pension on whether you wish to cancel the contract without penalty.

Then you need to find out whether he is an 'independent financial adviser' or a 'tied agent':

- An independent financial adviser in theory can advise you on the most appropriate arrangements available throughout the market. He is not connected to any one company, and is under legal duties to provide the best advice he can. It is difficult if not impossible to judge whether the advice is not tainted by thoughts of commission or is simply partisan or lazy or incompetent. But it does help if you can pay by fee rather than by commission given by the provider whose product he recommends; if you know how much he is earning through the advice he offers, and whether he would earn less by another route; what kind of back-up he has (access to research, perhaps through his firm or through a network or club of which he is a member which provides this kind of back-up); and what kind of qualifications he has (e.g. whether he specialises in pensions).

The problem with qualifications is that they are no guarantee – and that there is not one single widely recognised qualification which would give you comfort. The most common is the Financial Planning Certificate, but there are several levels of these, and a special supplementary exam in pensions. And many other certificates are available, run by the Chartered Insurance Institute, the Securities Institute, the Society of Financial Advisers or the Institute of Financial Planning. And they are of varying value. In any event, asking a financial adviser just what his qualification means can be deeply embarrassing, and even if he (or she) told you, you would hardly be the wiser. The best and most uncertain way is simply to ask around your friends, but that is also fraught. The answer is to acknowledge that you will never be sure, keep an open mind at all times, and brief yourself thoroughly rather than rely blindly on advice. Remember also that he has to eat as well; but whether he has to eat better than you is something for your own views to determine.

- Alternatively you may be approached by a company representative who works for and is paid by one company. If that company has just the thing you need, fine. And if its track record is up amongst the leaders, also fine. But you will not get a balanced view (although you might be lucky), and bear in mind also that a company rep gets a modest basic salary and then eats what he kills, i.e. the more he sells, the more he earns.

Often a tied agent cannot remember he is a tied agent and thinks he is an independent financial adviser; it is only when you see his card and it carries the logo of a provider, such as a bank or insurance company, that you may fully understand that he can only sell one company's services. And you will not learn what else is available on the market.

Saying 'No'

A good salesman will never take 'No' for an answer. While the excesses of the 1980s have been brought under control, you will not often realise how good a salesman is until after you have signed the contract. Pushy salesmen are relatively easy to deal with; if they are aggressive, you just say 'No'.

Saying 'No' to a skilled salesman who appears professional and skilled and is not selling anything is much harder. In all cases the following points are crucial.

- Bear in mind what you want, and reflect whether what you are about to buy is really what you need.

- Read (really read) the often very long letters that advisers are bound to send you before you sign up. There are usually two; the first is known in the trade as a 'reason why' letter. They have to set out the reasons why you need to sign up for something; if you sign without reading (or more sensibly understand the letter), you have only yourself to blame. If you cannot understand the letter, ask for it to be written in plain English, or don't sign. The second letter is a 'key features' document which sets out the main elements of the pension you are buying – as well as the commission that is being earned by your adviser. The point of telling you all this information is not to embarrass the adviser but to give you the context in which he gives you the advice.

- When working out what commission is being earned, bear in mind the up-front commission and then the annual commission payable every year thereafter, the extra commission payable if you increase your contributions in the future, and what the adviser will do in future years to deserve it.

Fee services

You might feel more comfortable with paying fees for advice, often on an hourly basis. The hope is that you get a more balanced view untainted by different commission rates offered by the various companies. The problem is paying the fees. Although they may be less in real terms (especially if you are paying in substantial amounts), they are not always easy to find. Commissions are deducted from your monthly payments so they come as less of a shock.

You might find it better to pay fees on top if you can afford it, since, if you buy a no-commission pension plan, your contributions will be worth more and increase more rapidly in value. You will not get tax-relief on the fees, and you will also have to pay VAT, but that is often a small price to pay for the added benefit.

Access to information

The quantity of offerings by the market is vast; no one adviser can possibly know all the products available, the details of such products (i.e. what is in the small print), whether the administration of company A is better than company B, or what the comparative charges or track records are.

Many have access to systems that can compare and contrast the various offerings; these are expensive to buy and not always easy to use and interpret. If your adviser is on his own (and not part of a network), he may not have access to these tools, and if he is with one company he certainly will not. On the

---

Table 23   What should I ask my adviser?

- Is my contract a single premium (more flexible) or an annual premium?
- How much (in £££) are you making out of this in the first year and in subsequent years?
- Would it be better to agree a fee scale with you?
- How are the charges paid: through the contributions (better for VAT) or by me (better for the tax-free roll-up)?
- What happens if I stop the contributions?
- What penalty applies (in £££) if I move to another provider in the first year or subsequent years?
- What are the provider's charges (in £££) in the first year and subsequent years?

other hand, it is easy to be blinded by print-outs and it is all too easy, by manipulating the data (e.g. using a different period of time for comparison), to show that one company or another is better over this period or that. Certain companies do have better reputations in the market than others, and by reading the press you can often get a feel of who is doing better than the others.

46 Tax relief

There would be no point in having a pension without tax relief; it would be more useful and efficient to simply save the money under the bed or in a bank. The main points of tax relief are:

- you only get tax relief up to the current maximum earnings

- you can get more tax relief the older you are

- you can use tax relief from other years if you haven't used them up already

- some of the relief can be used for life insurance or dependants' pensions.

How much tax relief do I get?

If the Inland Revenue can complicate things, they do. You only get tax relief on contributions on your first £87,600 (in 1997/8) of income; other years have different limits (depending on inflation). A table is set out in Appendix IV.

When do I get the tax relief?

If you are employed, you pay your contributions net of basic rate tax. The scheme administrator (usually the insurance company) then recovers the tax from the Inland Revenue and adds it to your pot. If you have paid higher rate tax, the difference between the actual rate and the basic rate is reclaimed later after you have completed your tax return and you get an adjustment to your coding. The system is known as PRAS (pension relief at source); it is better for you than an older system used for the former Retirement Annuity Contracts because you get the tax added even if you have not paid tax (perhaps because your earnings are too low)!

Tax relief on other years

If you didn't have the money in other years to pay, but are flush this year, you can use unused tax reliefs from other years, including up to six years before and one year ahead.

CARRY FORWARD OF UNUSED RELIEF

This allows you to use up missed contributions from earlier years. You use current tax rates, and you cannot use more than the tax relief available on earned income for the current year; you don't therefore get tax relief on payments over the level of taxable earnings.

If you pay more than the year's normal maximum contribution, then your inspector will automatically refer back over the last six years to discover any unused tax relief which can be carried forward. You have to fill in a special form (PP42) and send it to the tax inspector.

CARRY BACK

You can use up unused reliefs from previous years, if you want to pay in more in this year.

47 Trust: 'under trust'

One of those great mysteries of pensions jargon is the buzz-phrase of 'written under trust'. All it means is that if you die before you have taken all your benefits from the scheme, the money in the pension scheme does not go to your estate (where it would be added to all your other assets to see whether you have enough to have to pay inheritance tax) but to trustees (often the insurance company) who can use their own discretion as to whom to pay it to, although usually they will pay it to whomever you have indicated you would like it to go to.

Company Schemes

48 Abroad: what they do in other countries

We have suffered a great deal of criticism in recent years about the drawbacks to our pension arrangements. And they are by no means perfect: they are complicated, difficult to understand, expensive to administer and the marketing and distribution are imperfect. But the UK system has immense advantages – and our system is envied (with some exceptions) around the world. In fact, just as we are about to dismantle our system the rest of the world is rushing to copy it.

France, Spain, Belgium and other countries, which already have pension systems are trying to introduce company-backed, funded arrangements, just like company pension schemes. And Eastern Europe, with a clean sheet of paper, is doing the same. (see Table 24)

All these countries are cutting back on state pensions (either by raising the retirement age, increasing contributions or reducing benefits) and encouraging private pensions. Not all the private pension arrangements are working, sometimes because they are taxed or because there is nothing for them to invest in. But the objectives are there. And almost all the systems follow World Bank suggestions for a very basic state scheme, a compulsory private top-up and a voluntary top-up on top of that for those who want it. In particular they have devised protective systems to prevent government dipping into the pension pots, although they are not always fully effective, rather like in Britain.

See also OVERSEAS (page 143)

Table 24 Starting with a clean sheet: Eastern Europe								
	Hungary	Poland	Czech Republic	Estonia	Latvia	Slovenia	Romania	Bulgaria
Limited state pension system reform	✓	✓	✓	✓	✓	✓	✓	✓
Establishment of private pension funds	✓	✓	✓	✗	✓	✓	✓	✓
Shift to multi-pillar pension system	✓	✓	✓	✓	✓	✓	✗	✗
Public pension expenditure (% of GDP)	10.3	14.6	9.1	6.7	9.8	13.7	6.5	8.0
Year of latest pension expend-iture figure	1994	1995	1995	1995	1995	1994	1993	1995

✓ Changes underway or completed ✓ Changes planned ✗ No change

Source: World Bank. *Financial Times*, 19 August 1997

49 Accounts

All pension schemes must publish accounts every year. They are, in comparison with, say, company accounts, very simple to read and understand. They simply record how much money has come in, and how much has been paid out and where to.

There are now strict rules on the setting out of pension schemes accounts. There are several areas worth looking at.

- Expenses. These always look too high. However, running a pension scheme is not a cheap thing to do if you do it properly, and new legislation forces everyone to do it properly, if not too properly. There are administrators to pay, actuaries, lawyers, accountants and investment managers.

- Whether benefit payments are going up or down: this shows whether the fund is growing more 'mature', i.e. is beginning to have more pensioners than active (working) members. This means that the fund is more dependent on the assets in the fund than on future income from members and the employer.

• Whether the accountant is satisfied that the accounts have been properly kept during the year.

That is probably all you need to know; although post-Maxwell many people wish to know whether the accountant (or 'auditor') is also the same one as the employer's. Today, the accountant must have a contract with the trustees that sets out what he must do and not do – and ensures that any conflict of interest is identified; for example, whether the employer's contributions have been paid.

More importantly, the auditor has an obligation to inform (i.e. 'whistle-blow') to the Regulator (OPRA) if he sees anything that amounts to significant breach of the rules. This means that in practice anything significant will be reported at least by the year end.

The accounts have to be produced within seven months of the end of the scheme year, and there are penalties imposed on the trustees if they fail to ensure they are produced.

You are entitled to a free copy of the accounts on request not more than once a year.

50 Actuaries and their reports

More important in most cases is the actuarial report. In defined-contribution schemes the actuary's report is hardly significant, but in final-salary systems it tells you how well the scheme is doing, and whether there is enough money in the kitty to pay your pension if the employer fails. It will tell you:

• whether there is enough money to meet the minimum funding requirement, that is, the minimum required by law; that will guarantee around 60% to 80% of the benefits you expect in the worst case of poor performance

• whether the contributions have been paid by the employer and passed over to the fund as required

- whether the rate of contributions made by you and the employer is sufficient and certain assumptions as to future growth of the fund, future inflation and future tax rates. All these assumptions will in due course turn out to be wrong, but they will be reviewed every three years and over time should prove to be accurate.

- whether the investments are enough to meet the promise.

The trouble with most actuarial reports is they are written in a particular form of actuarialese, a language that few bother to penetrate. However, most have concluding paragraphs – and certificate or absence of certificates of adequacy of funding. What you are looking for is whether the assumptions that they have made as to the future are reasonable – and that the differences between the assumptions are reasonable. For example, if the actuary assumes that inflation is 5%, but that the income will be around 7%, then he is assuming a real yield, i.e. a return after inflation of 2%. That is a reasonable assumption, and reflects the historical performance of pension funds since the turn of the century. If, however, he assumes an inflation rate of 5% but a yield of investments of 8%, that is a real return after inflation of 3%, an optimistic assumption, and it means that he does not need as much money to be put into the fund, since he is expecting its returns to be higher. This is less cautious – though by no means unreasonable. However, it could mean the difference between solvency and deficit. The solvency and deficit statements in the actuarial report therefore must not be taken at face value (unlike the accounting report) and the assumptions have to be reviewed. The actuary is free within certain limits to set his own assumptions and usually does so after discussions with the employer (!) and the trustees. He must of course work within guidelines and Revenue limits.

The actuarial profession is a small one, of around 2,000 members in the UK, and very few have been criticised by their professional body over the years; unlike, for example, doctors, dentists, accountants and solicitors. Whether this is because they rarely do anything wrong, or because they are a closed community is not clear.

51 AVCs and FSAVCs

See CONTRIBUTIONS (page 121); TOPPING-UP (page 233)

52 Benefits: maximum

In company schemes there is a maximum level of benefits; there is no maximum with personal pensions (where the limit is on contributions). In most cases few scheme members achieve these maxima, either because they and their employers have not made sufficient contributions or because, through transfers, rights have ebbed away.

The main argument for limits is the tax relief available, which the Revenue think would result in abuse and tax leakage if no limits were applied. Some of these rules are extremely complicated and this guide does not attempt to set out, for example, the different rules that apply if you joined a scheme before 1987 or between 1987 and 1989.

Can I join or not?

You must be an 'employee' to join a scheme – this can include (genuinely) employed spouses of the self-employed (e.g. lawyers), part-timers or temporary workers, salaried partners and company directors.

But if you are self-employed, your only choice is a personal pension; this also includes you, if you are a consultant with income only from Schedule D, or a director of an investment company.

How much can I put in?

There are technical limits on how much either you or your employer can put in. You cannot put in more than 15% of your own income; and the employer is limited on how much he can put in, although few can achieve these limits.

When do I have to retire?

You normally have to retire between age 50 and 75 in the scheme although earlier ages are permitted in certain cases.

How much pension can I have?

The Inland Revenue limit you on how much you can have from a company pension scheme, and how fast you can earn pension rights. The normal maximum is two-thirds of your final salary; part of that can be reduced in exchange for a tax-free lump sum (commute) not more than one and a half times your final salary.

Of course, your scheme may not offer you that much; these are the maxima.

ACCRUAL RATES

How fast you can build up your pension is controlled by the Inland Revenue. You cannot, for example, build up your pension overnight. You are permitted to be awarded a pension of 1/60th of your final salary for every year of service, with a maximum of 40 such 60ths, i.e. a maximum of two-thirds of your final salary. If you only served 20 years, you would only have one-third of final salary.

Since few people (other than civil servants) maintain their career with one employer, and since transfer values rarely give year-for-year credits, it is possible to increase the rate of accrual in certain cases, if the funds are there. There are special rules if you joined your scheme before 1989.

WHAT CAN I USE AS 'FINAL SALARY'?

All these maximums are based on the use of final salary. The definition of final salary gives scope for a certain amount of planning if the funds are available to increase your pension; you can use normally any one of the last five years (including 'fluctuating emoluments', i.e. bonuses etc. averaged over three years). There are different rules for controlling directors.

You can use not only bonuses but also profit-related pay, overtime, commission, and benefits in kind (such as petrol or car expenses).

You cannot however (usually) use income or gains from shares, or termination payments (golden handshakes), except for death-in-service benefits; and if you joined the scheme after 1989 you cannot use more than the earnings cap (£87,600 in 1998/9) as final salary. The maximum pension you can enjoy at the moment from an approved scheme therefore is £58,400.

Table 25 How fast can I increase my pension rights?				
	Pre-1987 members		Post-1987 members	
Years of service	Fraction of final salary	Percentage of final salary	Fraction of final salary	Percentage of final salary
1	1/60	1.66	2/60	3.33
2	2/60	3.33	4/60	6.66
3	3/60	5.00	6/60	10.00
4	4/60	6.66	8/60	13.33
5	5/60	8.33	10/60	16.66
6	8/60	13.33	12/60	20.00
7	16/60	26.66	14/60	23.33
8	24/60	40.00	16/60	26.66
9	32/60	53.33	18/60	30.00
10	40/60	66.66	20/60	33.30
11	40/60	66.66	22/60	36.60
12	40/60	66.66	24/60	40.00
13	40/60	66.66	26/60	43.33
14	40/60	66.66	28/60	46.66
15	40/60	66.66	30/60	50.00
16	40/60	66.66	32/60	53.33
17	40/60	66.66	34/60	56.66
18	40/60	66.66	36/60	60.00
19	40/60	66.66	38/60	63.30
20	40/60	66.66	40/60	66.66

For pensions above these levels, you must either have been a member before the earnings cap applied (i.e. before 1987) or a member of a top-up scheme (see FURBs).

Finally, you can index-link the salary to get you up towards the earnings cap, so that each of your earnings in the last thirteen years is index-linked, and you choose the best three consecutive years and average those.

These limits include the benefits you have from other pension arrangements (known as 'retained benefits') such as any other company scheme, statutory scheme, personal pensions or Retirement Annuity Contracts, as well as certain overseas schemes.

The guiding principle, although the details are complex, is that no one should have a pension of more than two-thirds of final salary, the pension that the civil service is limited to.

Increases (augmentation)

You might be able to enjoy additional increases to reflect any rises in the cost of living up to the maximum two-thirds; indeed, pension schemes must now increase pensions by the lower of 5% p.a. or the increase in the cost of living (RPI). The index-linking is not applied to any lump sum you have taken.

Lump sums

One of the great advantages of a pension scheme, the 'much-loved anomaly' as a former Chancellor of the Exchequer called it, is the ability to convert some of the pension at retirement into cash, and tax-free cash at that. This is attractive, since the contributions that you and your employer have made have been tax-free, on the expectation that the Revenue would get its share when you took your pension and paid tax on it. The tax-free lump sum is a true tax benefit. It is therefore limited to one and half times your salary.

There are special rules if you joined the scheme before 1989; if you joined after 1989 the maximum in fact is the greater of

- 3/80ths of final salary (£87,600 in 1998/9) (i.e. £3,285) per year of service (i.e. £131,400), and

- the pension multiplied by 2.25, pension being the amount before any commutation or reduction in favour of spouses or dependants.

If you take the lump sum, then your pension is reduced using a 'commutation factor', often around 12:1, i.e. for every £12 of lump sum taken you lose £1 of pension, using unisex tables.

Death benefits

AFTER YOU RETIRE

You should be able to receive a pension for your spouse or your dependants once you die in retirement. The maximum is 2/3rds of your pension, i.e. 4/9ths of the final salary (but ignoring benefits from any other occupation). Such pensions can be index-linked at up to the cost-of-living. The indexation can be calculated as from your retirement date and not the date of your death.

Where there are several people enjoying a pension on your death, no one pensioner can enjoy more than the maximum of 2/3rds of your pension and the total maximum is the total of your pension.

The survivor's pension normally starts at the date of your death (unless you had a five-year guarantee on your pension, when it starts at the end of the guarantee period); and it can either continue until death or stop when the survivor remarries. If there is a remarriage, it will not normally restart if there is a divorce (or even if there is a nullity).

53 Benefits: statement

You are entitled by law to a statement of your company benefits at least once a year. The benefit statement must contain certain information (for details see INFORMATION AND DISCLOSURE, page 216).

54 Closure of my scheme

If your employer closes down, you will have many things on your mind besides pensions, employment being the main one.

But the closing of your employer (or insolvency) has repercussions on all your pension benefits, whether state or private. First, it will take a while (sometimes quite a while) to sort out the position of the scheme: who is entitled to benefits and how much they are and whether there is enough in the kitty to meet all the obligations.

This section looks at your position in relation to

- state benefits
- company benefits.

State benefits

CONTRACTED-OUT BENEFITS: FINAL SALARY SCHEMES

From April 1997 the contracting-out rules changed so that, by and large, employers could not buy back your SERPS equivalent benefits into the state scheme for you. But there is one major exception to that:

- the scheme must be in wind-up which started after April 1997
- the employer must be insolvent and unable to provide additional funds to the scheme
- the level of scheme resources (after any compensation payments) is such that its funding level is less than 100%
- the amount available in the scheme in respect of your rights is less than the amount which would have been available had the scheme wound up 100% funded.

Compensation payments are not made unless there has been some kind of fraud, so although the chance of buying back into the state scheme is rare, it will not be unknown.

The maximum benefits you will get if your scheme folds up other than because of fraud are the lower of:

- the amount required to restore your state benefits to a level that they would have been had you been contracted in, or
- the amount of accrued rights had the scheme wound up 100% fully funded according to the MFR calculation.

CONTRACTED-OUT BENEFITS: MONEY-PURCHASE SCHEMES

Similar rules apply if you are in a money-purchase scheme, with slight differences.

Company benefits

In most cases, you will be a member of a scheme, or series of schemes, retire, draw your benefits, and die, all without any difficulty. But sometimes life is not so simple. A major example of life getting complicated is when the employer goes out of business, or becomes insolvent and has ceased trading and a liquidator or receiver appointed. The pension scheme has to be closed; this is called winding up the scheme. The employer can no longer maintain the scheme, and the scheme needs to be closed down. This can be done in a number of ways:

● accepting that there are no new members, and no new contributions, and just running the scheme until the last member and beneficiary dies

● closing the scheme by buying benefits from an insurance company.

Which is the best buy is a matter for the trustees, acting on advice, to decide, and the pros and cons are for another book. But while the scheme is being wound up, your benefits can be quite badly affected.

● It will take quite a while to find out all the details the trustees need, including the lists of members, their data (sex, length of service, benefit levels, investment returns, etc.) and other liabilities. They will need time to check that all the contributions have been paid, and there are no hidden beneficiaries. In particular:

– the data has to be verified (such as joining the scheme)

– the DSS (if the scheme is contracted-out) has to be dealt with on the question of members' guaranteed minimum pensions or requisite benefits (i.e. equivalent state benefits)

– the receiver or liquidator of the company may need to claim from the state any employer contributions that were not paid in the final months of the company's life, and provide the necessary evidence, suffer a series of checks and certify the amounts

– the assets of the scheme need to be sold and converted

into cash, and this can take time, especially if property is involved

- getting decisions out of people can take time; many of them will wish to keep a low profile after a company collapse
- there may be complaints, or legal proceedings, to be dealt with before deciding how much money is available
- claims may need to be made from the Pensions Compensation Fund
- they may have to claim money from the DSS if there is not enough in the kitty.

So nothing will be decided in a hurry. Usually pensions in payment continue, and pensions falling due will be commenced; but transfers will usually be put on hold.

Once a receiver or liquidator is appointed, an independent trustee is usually appointed (unless there is one already in place). 'Independent' means that he or she has had no connection with either the employer or the advisers in the previous three years. The independent trustee is there normally to sort things out, since the normal trustees may often themselves have other concerns on their mind (perhaps because they have lost their job or are emotionally involved with the collapse, or may have had to move away).

The trustees sell the assets, put the money on deposit with a bank, calculate each member's entitlement and then see what it would cost to buy pensions from an insurance company. If the cost is too big (as can happen when interest rates are low) they may prefer to pay pensions out of their own assets instead. If there is enough money, fine; if there is not enough, they may have to scale down benefits or claim against the Pensions Compensation Board. If there is too much money, they (could) improve benefits or return the money to the company (and then on to the creditors). They will of course take advice at all stages – and they may (almost certainly) take advice and spend money on consultants. If there is a deficit in the fund, i.e. not enough money, this will be paid by you. Unless you are very concerned there has been fraud or maladministration you should be sparing in your demand for frequent information, for every time that you ask, it costs money that is paid for out of an inadequate fund.

If they pay out money too soon, they could overlook legitimate claims that have yet to be identified, and find they do not have enough to pay them. Sometimes it's worth asking (in cases of hardship) for payments on account if you are modest in your demands.

Meanwhile, simply tell the trustees where you are; if they do not have an up-to-date address, they can neither pay you nor tell you of developments, which they have to do every 12 months. And be patient: OPAS says that delays are rarely the fault of the trustees, who are normally looking after your interests.

OPAS (see ADDRESSES, page 254) has written a small manual to advise you what steps you could take to protect your position (and those of your colleagues) in these cases; it suggests that once you are aware that your employer (or former employer sponsoring the scheme of which you were a member) goes into financial difficulty, you should take the following steps.

- Call a meeting of the trustees to consider whether winding-up of the scheme should begin, and if so from what date. The date is important because if there are insufficient funds in the scheme, different people will rank in priority of getting their benefits secured. For example, pensioners usually get their benefits before deferred pensioners, so that if someone retires the day before the winding-up, they will be much better off than if they retired the day later.

- Ensure that all the advisers are aware of what is going on.

- Ask the trustees to write to all the members and former members telling them what is going on, giving a contact point for enquiries, informing them that death benefit cover (probably) no longer applies (you should probably take out your own cover) and that it will take some time to sort it out.

- Ensure that they also tell you what they are doing to collect unpaid contributions from the company (and from the government).

- Make sure that all the records are being brought up to date and that steps are being taken to give a rough estimate of the assets and liabilities of the scheme.

- Enquire what the trustees are going to do about people taking or wishing to take a transfer value – or who are about to retire.

- Question whether they are going to set up a consultative committee of members and pensioners (which can be a useful way of defusing tension and improving communication).

- Query whether the trustees are going to continue. Many may wish to pack it in, especially since it will be a traumatic time, but they should be encouraged to continue, perhaps with the backing of indemnity insurance against being sued.

- Check whether there is any control (and if so what) on the work of the independent trustee who must usually be appointed when a scheme closes down. The point of an independent trustee is to ensure that there is someone around to safeguard the interests of the members, because in previous times money was often removed from the scheme by liquidators. The problem nowadays is more that the independent trustee is so frightened of being sued that they over-administer the scheme, and spend more on winding-up the scheme than is justified by the amount of money in the scheme. Indeed, in some cases the money in the kitty can be spent all on administration and trustee fees so that there is nothing left for the beneficiaries. This is particularly the case in relation to appointments, oddly enough, by the Insolvency Service, the government department. So it is important to keep pressure on the independent trustee to be cost-efficient and not to spend, for example, so much money on establishing the position that there is no money left to pay pensions.

If there is not enough money to pay me in full

If there is not enough in the fund to pay you your benefits in full, there are several routes to put more money into the kitty.

- Claiming against the employer. The employer has a duty

to ensure there is enough in the pension fund to pay benefits, and must pay, over a reasonable length of time, any deficit. Of course, if he has gone out of business, there may not be enough to pay the deficit in part or in full.

- In many cases, the trustees of the scheme can claim against the Redundancy Fund operated by the Department for Employment, which will pay certain arrears of unpaid contributions.

- In some cases, if there is not enough to pay Additional Pension equivalents, the DSS will pick up the tab and restore payment of the SERPS pension.

- And if all else fails, there can be a claim against the Pensions Compensation Board.

Pensions Compensation Board

From April 1997 there has been a compensation scheme for occupational pensions, intended to compensate occupational pension schemes for losses due to dishonesty. The compensation scheme has no relevance to state retirement pensions or to a few schemes or types of schemes specifically excluded under the law. The Board is an independent body chaired by the Pensions Ombudsman with a member nominated by the CBI and one nominated by the TUC.

The PCB can pay compensation where an occupational scheme's funds have been reduced (after April 1997) only if there is a 'triple whammy'.

- Your fund has to be in deficit

- as a result of dishonesty, and

- the employer must be insolvent.

The maximum amount it will pay is 90% of the loss, and the PCB needs to be reasonably satisfied that the loss is the consequence of dishonesty, and not, just for example, poor investment or inadequate contributions. And the PCB needs to be satisfied that it is 'reasonable in all the circumstances' that compensation be paid. When it is paid, if it is, it is paid to the trustees and not to you directly.

The funds are raised by a levy on all other occupational pension schemes; it is applied for by your trustees, in writing, on a special form. When it gets a claim, the PCB acknowledges it, considers it, asks for more details, perhaps calls a meeting. Once it has made a decision to pay or not, it writes to the trustees setting out the decision – and its reasons. Where compensation is to be made, it will also set out the details.

It may take some time for the PCB to make a decision, but it can make interim payments even before its investigation is complete if it is satisfied that not to do so would cause hardship to scheme members. It can recover the payments once it has finished its investigation if it thinks it should.

There is no appeal against a decision of the PCB, but it will look again at an earlier decision if there has been a change in circumstances or new information has come to light. There may also be other reasons for a review of its decision.

If you are a trustee as well as a member once you have made an application the PCB will notify you that they have received it – and that they will look at it (or not, perhaps because your scheme is not covered); then it is passed to an Examiner for review.

The Examiner may ask for further information and documents either from you or other people, and may also ask for expert advice from consultants or actuaries. He will also liaise with the Occupational Pensions Regulatory Authority and any other regulators (including the police). The PCB will keep you informed of all significant developments which you should know about and report to you at regular intervals. You can amend or supplement information in the application at any time before a decision has been reached.

If you find it all too much or there is enough money in the kitty, you can withdraw the application at any time in writing, and the PCB can appoint a successor if it thinks it should. There is the opportunity (if it thinks it right) to have an oral hearing and it will give you 28 days' notice, and send you a note of the procedures to be followed. Fourteen days after the hearing the decision will be sent to you in writing, with reasons. The PCB does not make a final payment of compensation until it is satisfied that the trustees are unlikely to be able to make further recovery of assets.

55 Cohabitation

See GIRLFRIENDS AND OTHERS (page 141)

56 Contracted-out schemes

Contracting-out is largely dealt with in Section B (State Benefits). Whether your scheme provides what used to be known as Guaranteed Minimum Pensions, and now are called requisite benefits, depends on whether it has promised (in exchange for paying lower National Insurance contributions) to pay a pension broadly equivalent to the second state pension (SERPS). The decision is one for your employer and not for your scheme or you to make. You must however be told whether the scheme is contracted out or not.

57 Contributions

Very few of us have made full provision for our pension, and very few of us have exhausted our Revenue limits.

For those in employment it therefore makes sense, if there is any spare money about, to make additional contributions to those that you and your employer normally make.

These are commonly known as Additional Voluntary Contributions, because, as the advert for paint says, they are additional, they are voluntary and they are contributions.

AVCs

AVCs are a good thing, and you get tax relief on the payments you make; but they have their drawbacks too, and there may be alternatives which prove more attractive.

- AVCs receive tax reliefs when you put them in, but the benefits are taxable and must be used to buy an annuity on retirement (except those AVCs built up before April 1987). You no longer have to take your AVC benefits at the same time as your main pension.

- Tax is payable on the pension at the higher rate (currently for higher rate payers at 40%); but in practice your income may fall considerably and you may be paying a lower rate of tax (say, 23%).

- The maximum you can pay is 15% of pensionable salary up to £87,600 (i.e. £13,140); if you are already paying, for example, 5% to the scheme, you can pay another 10%.

- For some employees it may be more sensible to pay into an ISA (Individual Savings Account) instead. There is no tax relief on the contributions but the fund can be drawn tax-free and there is no need to buy an annuity. But if the money is used to buy an annuity, it is taxed less than a pension annuity, since only the income and not the capital return part is taxed. Voluntary annuities become more attractive the older you are: a 65-year-old will pay tax on 50% of the income while an 80-year-old pays tax on only 38%. But the maximum you can pay into an ISA is £5,000.

FSAVCs

In an AVC you make your extra contributions to the pension fund and they invest it for you. While they are required to keep a separate record of your contributions, they do not have to invest your contributions individually. Such a requirement would make a nonsense of the savings available by investing as a group.

You are free, though, if you wish, to pay your AVC contributions to another provider, such as an insurance company or building society; this is known as a 'free-standing' AVC or FSAVC.

AVCs normally have the advantage that the employer usually pays the overheads, whereas an FSAVC has to pay the overheads on the conventional money purchase scheme. In both cases the funds roll up tax-free.

Prisoners of the earnings cap can use AVC and also ISAs.

FSAVCs allow you to use your allowances to invest with the investment manager of your choice.

You should also make sure that your investments in AVCs are moved round as you get older, to make sure that increasingly the investments become less volatile, i.e. go up and down in value. So, some advisers feel you should ensure that your investments move more towards cash and bonds and more away from those investment managers who remain convinced that shares are the invariable answer.

FSAVCs allow you to choose your own investment manager. The way things are, this is a forlorn sport; you are bound, like every other investor, to look at history rather than present activity. It is in real life impossible to predict over the next year or decade who will be the best investment managers.

In practice, therefore:

- tax should not be the main factor driving your decision as to which way to go

- although the tax benefits differ (mainly in the time at which they are given), AVCs remain more attractive

- if you are subject to the earnings cap of £87,600, you might find your salvation by using your maximum AVCs and then using an ISA as a top-up.

Should I stop my AVC and start an ISA instead?

On an AVC (or FSAVC) you get tax relief on the contributions, but you have to pay tax on the benefits, and you cannot take the money in cash at the end (although you no longer have to take the benefits at the same time as your main pension). There may be a 'tax arbitrage' advantage, since you might be getting tax relief on contributions at 40%, but only paying tax on the income at, say, 23%. But both systems avoid tax on the increase in value and the income they receive.

Amount of contributions

You can pay £5,000 p.a. into an ISA. The most you can pay into an AVC/FSAVC is:

- a maximum of 15% of your pensionable salary (less the amount you are paying by way of regular contributions to the scheme). But you can pay contributions in respect of non-pensionable salary, such as bonuses and overtime.

- limited by the earnings cap (£87,600 in 1998/9), i.e. £13,140.

If you are capped then you could top up using AVCs and then (if you have the money) contribute also to an ISA.

GENERALLY

AVCs are usually better value than either FSAVCs or ISAs since the employer pays the overheads, which is a better benefit than even the tax recovery. If your contributions are only modest (say, £50 a month), an AVC is better value. But if you have an AVC and are paying more, it is probably not worth switching just for the marginal tax benefit.

INVESTMENTS

Most people who pay in AVCs are older than the general population; pensions become more important. If you only have five years or less before retirement, it would be sensible to move the investments from a pure equity (shares) or managed fund (unit trust type) into something a little less volatile, say, bonds, index-linked bonds or even property. And you need to check that the penalties for retiring early are only modest; some investment companies impose significant penalties on early retirement.

Voluntary and compulsory annuities

With some arrangements, you must use the money at retirement to buy an annuity (or pension). If you have to, you pay tax on all the regular annuity payments. If you have money that you do not have to use to buy an annuity, but you do buy one, you only pay tax on the income part of the annuity, not the return of capital that an annuity involves. In real life the difference is usually only modest, certainly for when you are younger. For example, if you are male and 65, you get taxed on 50% of the income, whereas if you are 80, you get taxed on only 38% of the income.

58 Controlling directors

If you are a controlling director (i.e. you and your family
control more than 20% of the company), you may be subject
to special restrictions on benefits and contributions. You are
likely also to be able to enjoy the benefits of a small self-
administered scheme. Your position is dealt with in Section
E, Higher Earners.

59 Death (mine)

Death is one of those things that few of us are keen to
contemplate. It is curious that while illness insurance is sold
as health insurance, death insurance is sold as life insurance.
But the death benefits can comfort your loved ones (or at least
your dependants) when you've gone. They can include:

- in company schemes, death-in-service cover. This means that
  the pension scheme will pay out a pension of up to two-
  thirds of the pension you could have received (i.e. about
  4/9ths of your income, i.e. roughly half) to dependants and
  in addition a cash lump sum up to 4 times your salary. The
  amount you get will depend on the terms of your own
  scheme.

- the cash does not normally form part of your estate for
  inheritance tax purposes. There is a curious route used to
  ensure that tax is not payable, through using trustees'
  discretion ...

Trustees' discretion

If you die while working, very often there is a cash amount
available from the scheme. You will have completed a form
before you die (sometimes known as a nomination letter) which
tells the trustees of the scheme whom you would like such
money to go to. Usually, of course, we do not know when
we will die, so the trustees merely file the letter and wait.

When you are dead, they will open the letter and discover
who you have decided should get the money. Oddly, they do

not have to follow your instructions. If, for example you have decided that your non-married partner should get it, but you still have a spouse (and dependent children), the trustees may consider applications from other people, including your spouse, to be considered to take the money.

The reason that the trustees have been given this discretion is curious; it is done so that you do not have the power to decide who gets the money. If you did have the power, it (the money) would be considered part of your estate, and you or your estate would have to have the money tipped into the pot for inheritance tax purposes. Giving the trustees this discretion gets it out of the inheritance tax problem – but it means that your wishes could be overridden on your death.

It is important therefore that you explain your position to the trustees in your nomination letter before you die, if you have an unconventional situation, and that you review the letter from time to time.

60　Death of my employer

See CLOSURE OF MY SCHEME (page 113)

61　Deferred members

Once you have left the scheme, you are called a 'deferred member', that is you have benefits left behind which you will collect when you get to the right age.

You must be treated fairly by the trustees as much as all the other members, so that you, as part of a group of similar members, must be considered for any increases that, say, working members enjoy, and you may in certain cases have the right to vote for members of the trustee board.

62　Deficits and surpluses

In final salary schemes, it is the duty of the employer and trustees to ensure there is enough money in the scheme to guarantee you will eventually get your benefits. There is now a requirement for minimum funding, introduced since April 1997.

But funding, ensuring there is enough money in the kitty, is an inexact science. Nobody knows for certain how much to put in to take account of your longevity (you do not know how long you will draw your pension for), your future earnings (you do not know what your earnings will be in, say, five or ten years' time, a figure you need to know to calculate how much pension you will get), or what inflation will be.

Because of these uncertainties, actuaries, the mathematicians that are employed to make a best estimate, re-calculate every few years how much there should be. But they inevitably get it wrong; either they are too cautious, in which case there is too much money in the fund (a 'surplus'), or too optimistic and there is not enough (a 'deficit'). Unless the scheme closes, neither condition is of any concern to you; all it means is that contributions will have to be varied in future, either up or down.

If there is a surplus, i.e. there is more than enough money in the kitty to pay your benefits, the employer can sometimes take a 'contribution holiday', i.e. he does not need to pay in any more contributions for a while, since he has clearly paid in more than he needed to in the past. (This description only applies to balance-of-cost schemes, where the employer promises to pay in a contribution which varies according to need, while you pay a fixed contribution.)

If there is a deficit, he will have to pay more in to the scheme over a period of years.

Recently there have been several court cases about whether surpluses (but never deficits!) belong to employers or scheme members. The law is quite complex; however, it is not possible any more for trustees to pay over surpluses back to an employer without an actuarial certificate saying it is safe to do so, the consent of the Occupational Pensions Regulatory Authority and telling the members.

63 Disability

It is against the law to discriminate against scheme members on the grounds of disability. However, some schemes may be unable to obtain cover at manageable rates if you have a particular affliction and there is no requirement for them to cover you at whatever cost.

For detailed coverage, see ILLNESS: SICKNESS AND DISABILITY (page 214).

64 Earnings and the earnings cap

Only a certain amount of your income, if you earn over £87,600 p.a., can be pensioned in a normal pension scheme. This limit is called the 'earnings cap', and it changes each year with inflation. If you do earn over this amount, see Section E, Higher Earners.

You also need to check how much of your earnings are pensioned. You can have at one extreme all your taxable income pensioned (including, for example, car expenses) or at the other extreme only your basic income. This can be unfortunate if most of your income is, say, commission or bonus.

How much of your income counts for pension is set out in your scheme booklet or annual statement, and it is crucial to check this from time to time to see if it is really what you want or agreed.

65 Employers, employment contracts and employer's duties

Giving advice on the scheme

If you are an employer, you might think twice about setting up a pension scheme; if you are an employee, you might wonder why the employer bothers. Employers establish pension schemes for the benefit of their employees; it would be surprising if they did not wish from time to time to extol the virtues of the scheme, or to persuade employees to join.

This was always thought to be a fairly innocuous pastime, indeed generally beneficial. When the Financial Services Act 1986 was introduced, it was clear that advice on occupational pensions was excluded.

However, many employees are now introducing group personal pensions, and these are usually considered to be investments covered by the provisions of the Financial Services Act, so that only authorised and trained people can advise on them.

The FSA came into force in 1988, and produced a large regulatory industry including regulatory bodies and controls on marketing.

Under the FSA anyone carrying on the business of giving investment advice or arranging deals in investments must be properly authorised to do so by one of the regulatory bodies. And if they are not, they commit a criminal offence. Most advisers are either independent (which is obvious) or tied, i.e. an employee of just one insurance company. However, a right in an occupational scheme is not an 'investment', and an adviser (whether independent or tied) has no interest in persuading people to stay in an occupational scheme. If an employer does not market his own scheme, no one else will – and meanwhile employees are subjected to pressures to either not join or make pension provision elsewhere. Therefore an employer can (and many people say should) give advice about an occupational pension scheme, whether money purchase or 'final salary'.

You can in particular give advice and information to employees:

- in relation to occupational pension schemes, in particular your own occupational scheme, and

- about personal pensions in general, provided you do not refer specifically to any particular personal pension scheme; general advice does not count as 'investment advice'.

Some people think you could even give advice on personal pensions because the question of authorisation only arises where you are 'in the business of giving investment advice' which clearly (in most cases) you are not. You do not, for example, receive commission or fees from giving advice; as the DSS says, if all you have to gain is a more contented work-force that does not constitute a commercial gain.

This means, therefore, you should be careful not to take any commission payment, or cut-price insurance policy, the provision of computer software to the company or the supply of lists useful to the company. And if you are in a group of companies that includes a pension provider (such as an insurance company) or tied agent, you should also avoid giving advice.

In other words you can give advice about:

- factual information about the terms and benefits of the various types of pension arrangements

- the relative merits of occupational pension schemes and personal pensions generally

- the merits of your own occupational scheme.

One of the major problems is helping employees who wish to opt out of the company scheme or transfer out of or into your scheme. It is therefore only proper to provide clear details of the company scheme (including who will pay the contributions and how much) and whether you as employer would be prepared to contribute to a personal pension scheme (not common). You could point out the disability provisions that your scheme offers (if any), which few personal pensions include – and that the overheads do not affect the value of a company scheme (normally) whereas they are highly material in a personal pension plan.

If an employee wants to take a transfer value from the scheme (less common these days, since many pension providers are uncomfortable about taking transfer values), you can advise the employee on the implications of taking a transfer, setting out clearly what the employee will be giving up. Government policy on this has reversed in the last ten years; at one time policy was to disapprove of such conduct. You could explain that the widow's benefits are preferable or that the revaluation arrangements are very attractive.

In particular you can advise on additional voluntary contributions (AVCs) since they are part of an occupational scheme – but not free-standing additional voluntary contributions (FSAVCs) since they are not part of the scheme and are covered by the Financial Services Act.

And you can, if you wish, refer the employees to an independent financial adviser to advise on the detailed financial advice that only an authorised person can give.

The major problem arises with Group Personal Pensions, increasingly popular for a variety of reasons. A Group Personal Pension (GPP) is a collection of individual personal pensions sponsored by a single employer, and, because they are personal, they are not covered by the Pensions Act 1995 (and the complex regulatory structure); but they are covered by the Financial Services Act, which has less impact on the management of the scheme but does contain, as mentioned, restrictions on the marketing and advice.

You can however (provided you do not accept commissions or another benefit) choose a particular GPP from a particular provider, and can

- negotiate terms with the GPP provider

- provide administrative assistance to the GPP provider, including collecting and forwarding contributions and notifying relevant changes, and

- arrange for a representative of the GPP provider to talk to your employees.

Any written details you provide to your employees about the GPP may fall within the FSA provisions on investment advertising, so that any documentation must first be approved by the provider of your GPP, when you can freely distribute it. Any literature notices or documentation should always be given to the GPP provider, such as advertising to the staff. Passing references in the report or accounts are not covered. Reduced rates of contributions (because you have negotiated a 'bulk sale' to the provider) are not covered – but you should not advise employees on which of the variety of investment funds they should select. You will need external advisers (if any) to help on this.

Generally

If you read the newspapers a great deal, you could be forgiven for considering, if you are an employer, that a pension scheme is the last thing you want. They can be expensive, difficult to control, lead to criminal and financial exposures and distract you from the proper business of business.

Yet still many employers continue and indeed establish pension schemes. Why do they do it? There are good reasons.

- A scheme relieves you from forms of blackmail by long-serving employees who become a grievous liability. Long-serving employees may seem a Victorian concept today, but in fact the much heralded mobility is far less widespread than thought.

- Pensions, if properly run and managed, are attractive to staff (the ones you want), especially if you want them to stay (and competitors may drive you to it).

- It is a useful stick to introduce good pensions for you and the rest of senior personnel. You might need more than one scheme (one for the fat cats and one for the plebs, but separate schemes, apart from FURBS, are rather rare and seen as undemocratic these days).

- Life cover, usually included in the provisions of a pension scheme, is a much appreciated benefit – and protects the firm against grieving widows besieging the directors' boardroom.

- Benefits can be paid which reduce the corporation tax and National Insurance contributions bill.

- They are one of the few tax-neutral arrangements still left alive.

- Even part-timers and contract staff welcome pensions as part of the package.

It is harder now to run a pension scheme than it was; and an employer will have to spend more time in managing a scheme than he did. But it is a harmless way of introducing worker-democracy through the back door (through member-elected TRUSTEES, see page 160).

Remember, however, the following if you are an employer.

- You cannot use any of the money in the scheme to invest back in the company or buy property of the company or shares in the company (small schemes excepted).

- You could use a small self-administered scheme to improve cash flow (see page 171) or invest back in the company.

- You can use the pension scheme to pass assets down the generations, i.e. transferring ownership without control, unlike the usual forms of trust, all of which have other drawbacks.

It is important if you sell the company to check that you do not also transfer control of your own pension fund, in the case where the majority of the fund is for your and your family's benefit.

66 Equal treatment: sex, disability, gays, lesbians

For many years, sex discrimination in pension schemes has been forbidden. It is not legal to have, for example, different retirement ages, or different eligibility (membership) requirements for pension schemes.

It is highly unlikely that your scheme operates illegal discrimination, but there are areas where differences for men and women are acceptable.

- It is still legal (unlike in the United States) to discriminate between men and women in relation to annuities. Because as a group women live longer than men, an amount of money will buy a lower pension for women (because it has to be paid longer) than for men. For odd reasons, company schemes cannot do this if the scheme is 'final salary', but can if it is money-purchase. Schemes can discriminate in the benefits they give to other groups: smokers, fatties or rock-climbers, for example.

- It is legal for an employer to discriminate against part-timers as part-timers but not on the grounds of sex; in practice, it is difficult for part-timers to prove discrimination.

- It is legal to provide 'bridging pensions', that is, a special pension to men under 65 to make up for the fact that (unlike women) they do not get the state pension until 65.

- There is a probable discrimination in all contracted-out schemes which provide benefits for men and women, but it is so complicated to explain to complainants and the judges, and no one knows what to do about it, that it is not worth complaining.

Other than that, racial discrimination is also illegal, although age discrimination is not.

Some of this law is UK law, some of it is based on European Union law. But wherever the law comes from, it is there to protect you. It has some rather special features, though.

- If you think you have been discriminated against, you must complain within six months of being aware of it.

- You can only claim for two years' worth of discrimination (with some exceptions).

- You cannot claim if the reason for the discrimination was not sex but something else (age, part-time employment, occupation) unless it is disguised (or 'indirect') sex discrimination.

- Racial discrimination in pension schemes is illegal (and rare, though not unknown).

You might feel that you have been discriminated against because you have been excluded from membership of the scheme, or benefits are different for one sex compared with another, or that retirement ages are different or that life cover is different. It is still permissible to offer MATERNITY (see page 223) benefits. If you feel you have been discriminated against, you should take advice, discuss it with your scheme manager or employer and, if all else fails, complain to an industrial tribunal or Pensions Ombudsman.

Part-timers

There have been a large number of court cases (many in the European Court of Justice) about whether part-timers are entitled to equal rights with full-timers in pension schemes. Since the mid-1970s it has been the position that it is illegal to discriminate between men and women in schemes, but it was only since 1986 that part-timers were held to be covered – provided it could be shown that discrimination against part-timers was based on sex discrimination.

If you have been working for an employer on a part-time basis, and there was a pension scheme which full-timers had the right to join, then it is possible that you could claim back-membership, perhaps as far back as 1976. That's the good news. The bad news includes:

- You have to show that the reason you were not permitted to join was not merely that you were a part-timer, but that the underlying reason was sex discrimination. The fact that most part-timers, for example, are women may be evidence of that.

- You have to show that you would have joined if you had had the opportunity. Until the mid-1980s, membership was often compulsory, but it was optional (by law) after that, and many part-timers refused to join because they didn't think it appropriate.

- You have to show that you have lost out. If you were only earning a modest amount, it is possible that you would only have earned the equivalent of the second state pension (SERPS) anyway, so that you would have earned very little, if anything, from membership of the company scheme.

- You have to make the claim within certain time limits, which could be as low as six months, from when you became aware you were discriminated against.

- It is possible you could only claim two years' worth of membership.

- The company must usually still be around to meet the claim; the claim is against the employer, not normally the pension fund.

- You may have to make backdated contributions for all those years to a contributory pension scheme (your union may lend you this).

Any claim would be made in either an industrial tribunal or with the Pensions Ombudsman, and if you are a member of a trade union, you may find it helpful to get them to back you. Putting a claim together could be complicated and expensive.

Because of a case at present before the courts, there are around 100,000 claims from part-time workers hoping to backdate their scheme membership. It could cost British industry around £10,000 million if the cases go ahead.

67 Finding my pension

One of the drawbacks of increased mobility of labour is the fact that many more people now leave benefits with their old pension scheme. The problem is that after many years you may have forgotten, like a squirrel, where you left that bit of your company pension. And even if you can remember, the company may have moved, changed ownership or changed names – or gone bust.

In many cases you will be entitled to a deferred pension right, i.e. a pension which is not payable until you reach retirement age.

Leaving your employer before April 1975

If you left your employer before April 1975, you almost certainly received a refund of your contributions, regardless of how long you had worked for the company. The exceptions are likely to be where you were made redundant or you left because of ill-health or where you decided categorically not to take a refund.

If your scheme was non-contributory (i.e. you made no contributions), then you will not have received a refund, and no benefits will have been retained for you (except in cases of redundancy or ill-health).

You will need to have kept some piece of paper, a certificate of entitlement to benefit or a letter from the scheme administrator given to you when you left, which sets out what you are entitled to. Without this you may have a problem making a claim. A simple certificate of membership will not do you much good; it doesn't say what happened when you left.

Leaving your employer between April 1975 and April 1988

If you completed less than five years' service in the pension scheme or were under 26 when you left, it is almost certain you took a return of contributions. If you think that you did not receive a refund, you will need to prove that you are entitled to a pension. Where the scheme was non-contributory then no refund will have been made and no benefits held for you (unless you left for ill-health or redundancy reasons).

If you did more than five years' membership in the scheme, you will probably be entitled to a pension even if you do not have documents to prove it. Paper makes it easier, of course.

Leaving your employer after April 1988

If you left the pension scheme with less than two years' service, you probably received a return of contributions. If you think that you did not receive a refund of contributions you will need to prove you are entitled to a pension. If the scheme was non-contributory then no refund will have been paid and no benefits held for you either. If you completed more than two years' service it's almost certain that you have some rights (the rules on all this are quite complicated and are known as 'preservation' in the UK, or 'vesting' in the US).

Making the claim

It is sensible (if you know who to write to) to write to the scheme administrator giving as much detail as you can (dates of birth, National Insurance number, dates of employment with the company).

If they refuse your claim, you can approach OPAS if you left either after April 1975 with five years' service or after April 1998 with two years' service. For free they will investigate your case. Without the paperwork, however, they might find it a bit of a problem.

And if you do not know where your pension scheme is, you can use the tracing service available from the Registrar of Pension Schemes.

If you transferred from your old scheme to your new scheme,

you have to add the service from the old scheme to the service in the new scheme to see if you qualify for a pension. If you left the receiving scheme prior to 1988 and your total combined service was less than five years, it is unlikely that you will have a pension.

If you think you were not given a refund, you may have had it in your pay packet although it may not have been separately identified. And it was the custom in those days to take the refund, even though with hindsight it was a mistake.

68 FSAVCs

See CONTRIBUTIONS (page 121)

69 Funding

Until recently (April 1997) there was no requirement that if an employer made you a pension promise, he had to set enough money aside to guarantee that promise in case he went bust and could not fulfil it. Following some scheme collapses this was thought no longer acceptable, and final salary schemes now have to have a minimum of assets to back the promises.

This requirement is known as the Minimum Funding Requirement (MFR). It does not guarantee that there will always be enough to pay out your benefits if the investments are very badly affected, or expenses mount up on a wind-up of the scheme, but over the next few years it should in most cases give you your benefits. But there is no guarantee (unless the money is stolen) so that if performance is inadequate, or the money is invested badly your pension may be affected. In the worst case it may bring your benefits down to 60% of what you were expecting, but it is an improvement on what went on before, and preferable to other guarantee arrangements in, say, personal pension schemes.

See also DEFICITS AND SURPLUSES (page 126)

70 Future developments

The only thing that is certain is that things will change radically over the next few years. The pensions industry cannot move for reviews, 'think tank' papers, discussion documents and policy studies.

So, long-term planning might be a little difficult. Futurology is a fool's game, but the government has already announced the end of PEPs and TESSAs, to be replaced by Individual Savings Accounts, particularly designed for the lower paid.

The fiscal neutrality of pensions has already been attacked by the government when ACT was withdrawn. The impact of the tax changes was significant.

Table 26 What the withdrawal of Advance Corporation Tax means to your money-purchase pension

Reduction in fund value

Term to retirement	Fund value at retirement		Reduction in fund value
	Before	After	
10 years	£19,100	£18,700	2.3%
20 years	£64,300	£61,000	5.0%
30 years	£171,400	£157,300	8.2%

Increased contributions

Term to retirement	Monthly contributions	
	Before	After
10 years	£100	£102.36
20 years	£100	£105.32
30 years	£100	£108.96

Impact of existing savings

Term to retirement	Existing fund value	Fund value required (%)	Additional single premium	Additional monthly premium
10 years	£100,000	4.2%	£4,224	£23
20 years	£50,000	8.6%	£4,315	£7
30 years	£10,000	13.2%	£1,321	£1

Source: Scottish Equitable

And we all know that the state scheme is due for a radical overhaul.

If you would really like to read some thinking on future policy, and whether we will copy the Australians (who make everyone contribute 10% of their income, but allow them to take it all in cash at retirement), or the Chileans (who have reconstructed their country using compulsory pension contributions, but cover only half the workforce), or the Singaporeans who invest a great deal of the investments in public housing and pay a return of only half the market rates (in other words, tax the pension scheme), or the now deceased New Zealand system, which gives no tax relief at the beginning but allows you to take the pension tax-free, we will have to see.

Lots of bodies, including the Consumers' Association, the National Association of Pension Funds, most of the 'think tanks' and others have suggested there should be major reforms to pension arrangements. Most of the complaints are about unfair tax treatment, excessive complexity and unreasonable restrictions. The government has now instituted a Pensions Review to look at what to do.

EMU

It may be that in due course the UK will join the European Monetary Union (EMU) and use a European-wide currency. Will this make much difference to pensions? It will probably make little difference to the day-to-day pensions or benefits. But it will have some indirect effects.

- Your underlying assets will probably be spread wider in overseas stock markets and assets.

- Foreign pension funds will find Britain a more attractive place to invest; at the moment many of them are prevented from investing here.

- Foreign government pension liabilities which are unfunded are likely to have an impact on the value of the currency and may lead to slightly increased inflation.

71 Girlfriends and others

This section is slightly sexist; it should also read 'boyfriends and same-sex friends'. Whatever your partner position, if you and your partner are not married, you may have a problem in ensuring that your partner receives the normal spousal benefits such as death-in-service insurance, or a spouse's pension.

The system finds it more difficult to cope with such relationships, because of the problem of finding out just what that relationship was. In practice, many schemes give discretion to trustees to pay certain benefits to partners but they will need to discover information about the degree of dependency (financial or otherwise) which they do not need to do with married couples.

72 Ill-health benefits

See DISABILITY (page 127)

73 Indexation

Your pension must be indexed both after you leave the scheme and once you have retired. The law only applies to benefits you have accrued after April 1997, but most schemes apply the principle for earlier years. The minimum is the retail price index up to 5% a year.

74 Joining the scheme

Almost anyone who is an employee can join a company scheme if there is one and they let you join. That includes you if you are a director (whether controlling or not), a part-time or temporary employee, an employed spouse, a salaried partner or a UK resident of an overseas employer.

However, certain people are not eligible, even if both you and your employer are keen to see you join: you cannot join if you are regarded as self-employed, a director of an investment company or a consultant.

75 Leaving the scheme

You have the right at any time to leave a scheme; the former rules that an employer can force you to join were repealed some years ago. However, it is likely that employers will in future be given the right to compel you to join a scheme.

When you leave the scheme (whether or not you leave the employer), you have the right to leave your benefits there, or take a transfer payment to another pension scheme, which can be an occupational pension scheme or a personal pension.

You should not normally leave your company pension scheme unless there are special reasons to do so (such as, you are making significant contributions to a personal pension, or you are staying with the firm for only a short time).

See also TRANSFERS (page 244).

76 Membership and eligibility

Who can join the scheme depends on the rules of the scheme and the wishes of the employer. It is however illegal to discriminate on membership on the grounds of sex, disability, length of service or race, but not on the grounds of age.

77 Overseas

For some, moving overseas is a very sensible option: better weather, better food, and perhaps the children growing up there are all good reasons – as well as the fact that in some places it might be cheaper to live, important when on a restricted income.

Retiring overseas

STATE PENSIONS

If you retire and decide to move somewhere warmer and more congenial, the state pension can cause a bit of a hiccup. Normally you can continue to receive both your Basic State Pension and the SERPS pension, if any, and it will be payable overseas. But if you say you are living outside the European Union, it will not be uprated in line with improvements in the UK but will remain fixed at the same rate as when you left. There are several solutions to this problem.

- Come back from time to time, and re-establish the new level of state pension before returning overseas. This could be expensive once the air fares are taken into account, and you need to have re-established residence in the UK for it to be effective (i.e. stay quite a while), so probably not a thing to do just to improve the pension.

- Have the funds paid in the UK, and then sent on; there will of course be bank charges, and you will be liable for UK tax on other income, but maybe it is something to consider.

- Move to a country which has an agreement with the UK on improving pensions; Table 27 sets out the countries which have an agreement.

Table 27 Countries (non-EU) where you can get an annual increase to your UK state pension

(DSS leaflets in brackets)	
Barbados (SA43)	Israel (SA14)
Bermuda (SA23)	Jamaica (SA27)
Bosnia-Herzegovina (SA17)	Jersey (SA4)
Croatia (SA17)	Malta (SA11)
Cyprus (SA12)	Mauritius (SA38)
Federal Republic of Yugoslavia (SA17)	Philippines (SA42)
Former Yugoslav Republic of Macedonia (SA17)	Sark (SA4)
Guernsey (SA4)	Slovenia (SA17)
	Switzerland (SA6)
	Turkey (SA22)
	USA (SA33)

If you are going abroad for more than six months, Retirement Pension or widows' benefits can be paid anywhere in the world. If you go abroad permanently, you do not get annual increases unless you live in a European Union country, or certain other countries. There are special payment arrangements if you go to Pakistan, India, New Zealand or Bangladesh (leaflets available from 0191 218 7777).

Otherwise:

- If you are away for three months or less:
  - if you are currently being paid direct to a bank or building society, this continues, or
  - if you are paid by order book, the orders remain valid when you return to the United Kingdom and you can cash them then.

- If you are away for four, five or six months:
  - if your state pension is paid into a bank or building society account, the payments continue, and you are free to make your own arrangements to transfer the payments abroad, or
  - if you are paid by order book, when all the orders up to the date of your departure have been cashed, return your order book to the nearest DSS office, and consider having payments then made to a bank or building society account. Otherwise, it will accumulate and all arrears will be paid to you in a lump sum when you return to the UK.

- If you are away for seven to twelve months:
  - if you are currently being paid direct to a bank or building society in the UK, you can choose whether to continue with this arrangement, or
  - if not, a sterling payment cheque can be sent direct to you, your overseas bank or an agent, at the end of every 4 or 13 weeks, or
  - you can leave your benefit to accumulate and it will be paid to you in a lump sum when you return to the UK.

If your weekly rate of benefit is £2 or less and is paid to

you annually, this method will continue while you are abroad.

In any event, you should write to the DSS Pensions and Overseas Benefits Directorate (see ADDRESSES, page 257) well before you leave and get the forms, which should be returned before you go abroad.

- If you decide to stay abroad permanently, or for more than 12 months:
  - your pension will be paid by automated credit transfer to your overseas bank account where this is possible
  - where it is not possible to pay direct, a sterling payment cheque will be sent at the end of every 4 or 13 weeks either:
    - (a) direct to you or your overseas bank, or
    - (b) direct to a person or agent outside the UK nominated by you.
  - If you are currently being paid direct to a bank or building society in the UK you can choose:
    - (a) to continue with the arrangement, or
    - (b) to leave the benefit to accumulate to be paid in a lump sum when you return – provided you are away for no more than two years.

It may take a while for the first payment to be made; in any event the DSS Pensions and Overseas Directorate should be contacted well in advance (see ADDRESSES, page 257) and the forms filled in and returned.

WIDOWS

If you are entitled to a Widow's Payment (see page 61), it can be paid to you anywhere abroad, but if your husband died while you were both abroad you can only get Widow's Payment if

- your husband met the National Insurance conditions for Widow's Pension or Widowed Mother's Allowance, or

- if you return to Great Britain within four weeks of his death.

Provided you have made the right NI contributions, your residence abroad will not affect any claim you make when you return to the UK.

You may be able to get a Widow's Pension if your husband dies and had paid NI contributions. You cannot get Widow's Pension and Widowed Mother's Allowance at the same time.

To get Widow's Pension at the full rate, your husband will have had to have maintained a full (or almost full) NI record while he was working (see page 52). You can claim your Widow's Pension from abroad, by writing to the Benefits Agency (Pensions and Overseas Benefits Directorate. The benefit can normally be paid anywhere, but it will not receive annual increases unless you live in

- one of the countries set out in Table 27 above

- an EU country or EEA country (Table 28).

Table 28 European Union and European Economic Area countries		
European Union:	Luxembourg	an EU country, and by EU countries as part of the UK.
Austria	Netherlands	
Belgium	Portugal	
Denmark	Republic of Ireland	
Finland	Spain	*European Economic Area:*
France	Sweden	
Germany	UK	Iceland
Greece		Liechtenstein
Italy	Gibraltar is normally treated by the UK as	Norway

You can receive your Widowed Mother's Allowance anywhere if your stay abroad is temporary. If you are living abroad and your child normally lives with you, you can get the increase in benefit for your child only if you live in certain countries (including the EU and EEA).

War Pensions

War Disablement Pensions and War Widow's Pensions can usually be paid anywhere in the world and the right to a War

Pension does not depend on the payment of NI contributions. If in the past you received a War Widow's Pension which was withdrawn when you remarried, that pension may be restored if you have become widowed again, divorced or legally separated. If you receive a War Pension and intend to live permanently abroad, you should inform the War Pensions Agency (see ADDRESSES, page 257).

OTHER BENEFITS

Whether you get other social security benefits when retiring abroad is a complex question and outside the scope of this book; a range of leaflets is available from the Benefits Agency, covering a wide range of countries including those in the EU and EEA.

PRIVATE PENSIONS

Private pensions will, oddly, retain their UK value because, provided inflation is under 5%, the law is that they must be index-linked (if an occupational scheme). Other pensions depend on the deal you have done with the pension provider. Tax will be deducted at source.

Working overseas

It is sometimes not very certain that you will return, or when you will return to the UK when you go abroad, however certain you are at the outset. So, the question of whether you should retain cover when you go abroad is a sensitive one. The general conclusion is that, unless there are very good reasons not to, it is normally sensible to continue paying NI contributions when you are abroad, in order to maintain and improve pensions coverage from the state, however modest that state pension is.

If you decide to continue to pay NI contributions (even when you do not have to; you have to if your employer has a place of business in the UK, if you are ordinarily resident in the UK and were so just before you started working overseas), you can pay:

- Class 2 contributions (whether you are employed or self-employed), provided you have lived in the UK for at least three continuous years (or paid a certain amount in NI contributions), and you are working abroad but not liable to pay Class 1 contributions and

- – were employed or a self-employed earner in the UK just before you went abroad, or
- – you would normally be employed or self-employed, but were unemployed just before you went, or

- Class 3 Contributions (voluntary contributions) which are a little less; they do not however maintain health cover abroad.

Either way, you have to pay the contributions within 42 days of the end of the tax year; late payments will prejudice your benefits. And you cannot pay contributions more than six years after they were due.

You can pay either by direct debit from a UK or Channel Islands bank or building society account every four or five weeks; there is a form (CF83) at the end of leaflet NI38 which enables you to do that. Alternatively you can pay annually, and the Contributions Agency will send you a bill each year, or get someone else to pay for you.

All these steps should ensure that you continue to earn state pension credits while you are overseas; you may also (almost certainly will) have to pay local social security contributions as well, so it may be an expensive option. You are not supposed to (and it is probably not worth it) pay double social security contributions if you are in another EU country (see below).

European Union

Every EU country has its own rules, which you need to follow before you can get a pension. The age at which you get a pension varies from country to country. You can claim your pension directly from any EU country that you have been insured in. Or you can claim from the EU country you live in when you are getting near pension age. If you have been insured in the UK, the DSS will normally send you a claim form about four months before you reach retirement age. The form asks you whether you want to claim a UK Retirement Pension, and whether you have been insured in any other country. It is important that you keep the DSS notified of your present address otherwise they cannot trace you.

If your husband dies when you are in one EU country but he was insured in another EU country, you can claim widow's benefits in either of the countries.

If you claim Retirement Pension or widow's benefits in the EU country where you live, that country will pass on details of your claim to any other EU country where you (or your late husband) was insured.

WHAT HAPPENS THEN ...

Each EU country where you have paid insurance towards a pension will look at your insurance under its own scheme and work out how much pension you can have. As long as you meet the rules, you will get a pension from each country.

Each country will also look at any insurance you have in another EU country if this can help you to get a pension – or a higher pension – under its own scheme.

The way this works is that each country sends details of your insurance record to the others. Each country then works out how much to pay you, in two ways.

- Each country works out how much pension you can get, just from what you have paid into its own social security scheme.

- Each country adds together your insurance in all countries, then each one sees how much pension you would get if your insurance had all been paid into its own social security scheme. But each country only has to pay you part of this; how much it pays you depends on how much you have paid into its scheme.

While the second calculation is performed (it may take some time), you get the pension calculated under the first one. If the second one gives you more, you get the second one.

How is it paid?

Each EU country decides how it will pay your pension; if you are in the UK you can be paid a pension from any other EU country (which may affect your other social security benefits, such as Income Support). And you can be paid a UK Retirement Pension (plus the extra if you are over 80) in any other EU country. It can as before be paid into a bank or building society account either in the UK or abroad. Back payments that you are entitled to will normally be paid straight to you. Unless you are in the UK and there are back payments from another EU country and you get Income Support, the DSS will deduct its Income Support payments from the back payments. A similar deduction applies by other EU governments.

If you get a pension from any EU country, you can also be paid extra for any adult who is dependent on you, even if the adult is in another EU country. In relation to child dependants, if the EU country you live in pays you a pension, it should pay you the benefits for your children too (based on the terms of its own scheme); you may get Child Benefit or extra pension for the children or both.

If you do not get pension in the country where you live and you and your spouse are not working, the benefits for the children are paid either by the country that you get a pension from, or if you get a pension from two countries the country where you were insured for the longest time. If you are a widow with children, and your husband was insured in only one EU country, that country pays the benefits for a child; it works out what the benefits are, using its own rules under its own scheme (they could be child benefits, orphan's pension or extra widow's pension, or a combination of any of them).

If your husband was insured in more than one EU country, it will usually be the country where the child lives that pays the benefits. However, your husband must have been insured in that country and there must be some benefit paid for the child.

If your husband has not been insured in the country where the child usually lives or that country cannot pay any child benefit, the EU country where your husband was insured the longest has to pay the child's benefits.

S.615 plans

If you are an expatriate, you might find that a 's.615 plan' is attractive and preferable to an offshore plan. UK (and non-UK) corporations often provide retirement benefits to their expatriate employees through an offshore plan. The offshore plan is usually located in a tax haven in order to avoid local tax on investment income, contributions and benefit payments. An alternative to an offshore plan with equivalent tax advantages is a so-called 'Section 615 plan'. This is a UK plan approved under Section 615 of the Income and Corporation Taxes Act 1988.

Requirements

A Section 615 plan is a pension plan set up under irrevocable trust in the UK for overseas employees only.

- The plan benefits may follow the overseas pattern but may not be grossly excessive.

- The plan must have for its sole purpose the provision of superannuation benefits in respect of employment wholly outside the UK. Duties performed in the UK that are incidental to the performance of duties outside the UK must be treated as performed outside the UK.

- The plan must be recognised by the employer and the employees in the trade/undertaking concerned.

- The trustees must be UK-based.

UK taxation of Section 615 plans

- Investment earnings receive the same reliefs afforded to individuals not ordinarily resident in the UK. In particular, capital gains tax is avoided and tax is not levied on dividends from certain government bonds or overseas investments.

- UK corporate contributions to a Section 615 plan are deductible.

- Benefit payments (pensions and lump sums) are paid gross to non-UK residents (lump sums paid to UK residents may qualify for tax relief, at least in part).

BENEFITS FOR AN EMPLOYER

The tax treatment of an offshore plan and a Section 615 plan is likely to be the same. In addition, both offshore plans and Section 615 plans avoid you being subject to the 'UK earnings cap', i.e. the tax limits on contributions in respect of salary over a certain amount (£87,600 in 1998/9). However:

- The administration of a Section 615 plan is potentially much easier – the trust document and administration is provided in the UK, and there is no need for an interface with overseas administrators and trustees. In effect, the Section 615 plan can be run alongside the main UK scheme.

- Since Section 615 plans are established in the UK, there is a greater chance that contributions to such plans will avoid treatment as a benefit in kind, as a result of double-tax treaties between the UK and other countries.

- Similarly, double-tax treaties may enhance the prospects of a Section 615 plan recovering overseas withholding tax.

In addition:

- Special one-off plans may be established on an individual basis at a low cost compared to the cost involved in the establishment of a one-off offshore plan.

- An individual may have concurrent membership of a Section 615 plan and a UK-approved scheme subject to certain conditions (i.e. membership of two tax-advantaged pension plans).

SHOULD I STAY IN THE NORMAL UK PLAN?

Under certain circumstances, you could as an expatriate remain in the normal UK approved plan.

- If you are directly employed overseas by a UK employer, you may remain indefinitely in the UK approved plan.

- Subject to certain conditions, if you are employed overseas by an overseas employer, you may remain in the UK approved plan for up to 10 years providing there is a definite expectation that you will return to/retire in the UK.

Staying in the UK approved plan cuts the administrative

inconvenience and cost of setting up a new plan and could also avoid fragmentation of benefits.

However, there are some cases where you will not fulfil the above criteria. For example, if you are employed by an overseas employer with no intention of returning/coming to the UK, a Section 615 or offshore plan might be appropriate for you.

Even where it is possible for you to stay in the UK plan, an employer may wish to provide different benefits for its expatriate employees; perhaps UK social security may not apply and the benefit formula in the UK plan may be inappropriate. Alternatively, an employer may wish to avoid the application of the UK earnings cap or benefit limits, or indeed may wish to impose a longer vesting period than would normally be allowed in a UK approved plan. This can be achieved by setting up a Section 615 or offshore plan either to supplement or replace the UK approved plan benefits.

Receiving a pension from overseas

You will normally be taxed on only 90% of the pension you receive (ICTA 1988 s.65(2) under Schedule D Case V) unless the overseas scheme becomes registered as approved by the Inland Revenue (which happens occasionally with Irish Republic schemes) when PAYE will be deducted.

Going to … Australia?

There are some countries which are particularly attractive to you if you want to take your pension overseas.

If you transfer to Australia, for example, you would have to pay tax at your top rate (with a maximum of 48.7%) on the growth of the fund from the time of becoming an Australian resident to the time of transfer. Accordingly it is important to arrange the transfer as soon as possible; in fact, if the transfer is made within six months of becoming a resident, there is no tax penalty. There are pension arrangements (called superannuation in Australia) which are recognised by the UK Pension Schemes Office which will accept UK transfers. And what is not mentioned is that usually the benefit is paid in tax-free cash – there is usually no need to take the benefit in pension form.

See also ABROAD (page 105)

78 Part-timers

See EQUAL TREATMENT (page 133)

79 Pensions Compensation Board

See CLOSURE OF MY SCHEME (page 113)

80 Pension Schemes Registry

One of the problems thrown up by several studies by the now defunct Occupational Pensions Board over twenty years ago was that many people found it increasingly difficult to remember where they had left their pension when they changed jobs perhaps many years previously. The ideal solution was a registry where there were records of all pension schemes (including their rules and accounts) and complete details of membership. A similar sort of registry already exists to manage the National Insurance Fund; but it requires 12,000 civil servants to run it and the original plan proved just too expensive. Some years ago a much simpler registry, now called the Pension Schemes Registry (see ADDRESSES, page 257) was set up, but it simply records the names of companies sponsoring pension schemes, and what happened to them; for example, whether they closed down, were taken over or dissolved and who, if anyone, is now running that scheme and what their address is. It carries out thousands of searches every year (which are free) most of which it records as 'successful', but it is not clear what success means here; certainly it is true that it is a somewhat blunt weapon to try to trace the sponsor of your company pension scheme from twenty years ago. At least it is better than nothing and can sometimes help you on the way to track what might be quite a chunky benefit.

The Registry now provides a tracing service to pension scheme members so that you can try to find out about schemes you may have been a member of, but cannot now find. It is based in Newcastle and it also collects a couple of levies or taxes from pension funds each year.

- A levy to pay for the Pensions Compensation Fund; the Compensation Levy funds compensation payments to pension schemes who have had their money stolen. The amount of the levy is modest, just 23p per member per year. Why it is 23p nobody knows, especially since (at the time of writing) there has been no claim against the fund, and it has the power to borrow to pay out if it needs money. Only occupational pension schemes pay this part of the levy – only they can claim against the fund. Personal pension claimants have to claim elsewhere.

- A levy to pay for the supervision of pension schemes (the Occupational Pensions Regulatory Authority, Occupational Pensions Advisory Service, Pensions Ombudsman etc.).

See also FINDING MY PENSION (PAGE 136)

81   Redundancy and unfair dismissal

If you are made redundant, you may have some of your redundancy pay diminished if you are soon to be eligible for a pension. Otherwise when you make your claim for redundancy pay, you should check whether there is anything extra to pay in respect of pensions (usually not).

If you have been unfairly dismissed, you may be entitled to an award; you will always need to consider whether you can add to the claim for loss of future pension rights. The amount involved is often enough to put the claim at the legal maximum.

There are special leaflets (see Appendix III) which explain your rights on redundancy.

82   Retirement ages

Until the turn of the century, no one had a retirement age. You worked until you dropped; some people feel that even today the fact of working helps to keep you alive. It was not until the first state pension began in 1908 that the idea that someone had the right to stop work after a certain age became widespread. Not only that, but employers seized on the idea to dispose of workers who had become less effective. It therefore suited everyone that there should be a retirement age.

The question nowadays is not so much whether there should be a retirement age (although there is some thinking that suggests we should do away with it) but what that age should be.

Most begin with the state pension age, that is, the age at which the state begins to pay the state pension (although, as we have seen, the value and importance of the state pension is bound to decline a great deal). The state pension age for men and women is 65, although women may retire earlier, as follows:

Table 29   Phasing-in of equal state pension ages for women

If you are a woman, and

- were born during or before March 1950, your retirement age is 60
- were born during or after April 1955, your retirement age is 65.

Otherwise, your retirement age is set out in the table:

When you were born	Your pension age (year and month)	Pension year
April 1950	60.1	2010
October 1950	60.7	2011
April 1951	61.1	2012
October 1951	61.7	2013
April 1952	62.1	2014
October 1952	62.7	2015
April 1953	63.1	2016
October 1953	63.7	2017
April 1954	64.1	2018
October 1954	64.7	2019
April 1955	65.0	2020

If you are a woman and think this unfair, especially if you have planned your retirement on the basis of retirement at 60, you should thank your lucky stars the government did not go for 67, which is what it should have done. In due course it is inevitable (if the state pension survives) that it will not be paid until age 70, which takes us back to 1908 which is what it was then. The reason however will be different; the reason then was that relatively few lived past 70, so it was cheap; the reason in the future is that too many live way past 70.

You may wish to plan your retirement date to coincide with that of the state pension age (and indeed if you are employed, it is possible that your employment contract reflects the state pension age), but of course you do not have to. You can stop work whenever you like, if you can afford to. The difficulty is knowing what age is the best one.

The decision may of course be taken out of your hands; or you may decide after your formal retirement to continue working part-time or even full-time, or for another employer or in a lighter job. Most people feel they would like to continue doing something, and they usually feel the better for it.

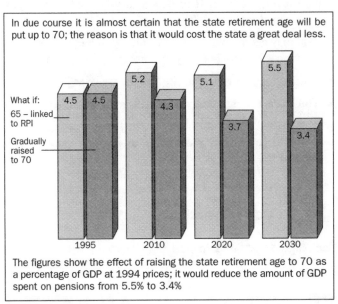

In due course it is almost certain that the state retirement age will be put up to 70; the reason is that it would cost the state a great deal less.

What if:
65 – linked to RPI
Gradually raised to 70

4.5 4.5   5.2   5.1   5.5
          4.3   3.7   3.4

1995   2010   2020   2030

The figures show the effect of raising the state retirement age to 70 as a percentage of GDP at 1994 prices; it would reduce the amount of GDP spent on pensions from 5.5% to 3.4%

Figure 14 Will they change state retirement age to 70?
Source: OECD

83 Retiring

This is not a book about retiring; there are plenty of good ones available. But a summary of some of the options may be useful:

- You will get the Basic State Pension (or some of it) or a Widow's Pension.

- You will get a second state pension (if you were employed or married to someone who was employed) either from the state or from a private arrangement.

- You may get a tiny amount from an old state scheme, the graduated scheme.

- You may get Income Support if the pensions are not sufficient.

- You can get Housing Benefit if you need help to pay your rent.

- You can get Council Tax Benefit if you need help to pay the council tax.

- You may get an invalidity addition if you had an invalidity allowance shortly before you reached retirement age.

- You will get an Age Addition if you are over 80.

- You can get some payments if necessary from the social fund to help with short-term needs.

- You will get whatever company or personal pension you are entitled to.

84 Sex discrimination

See EQUAL TREATMENT (page 133)

85 Take-overs

The reduction of mergers and acquisitions after the recession seems now to be over; companies are being bought and sold all the time. And if you are working for one that is bought, there can be a *frisson* of concern about the pension arrangements.

The pension rights that you have built up to date cannot be touched (although, see DEFICITS AND SURPLUSES, page 126).

But most companies would not be human if they did not want to clean up the pension arrangements and perhaps bring them into line with their own. Or you may be transferred to the new employer's pension scheme if what the buyer has bought is not the company but the business or part of it.

You are normally offered three main options.

- You would be invited to join the new scheme. Sometimes (increasingly) this will be a money-purchase (defined contribution) scheme; and

- either transfer your accrued rights into the new scheme, perhaps with enhanced terms to persuade you to join; or

- leave your benefits where they were.

Most companies will use extensive communications to explain what is going on and what the options are. The only thing to worry about is whether the existing rights are preserved (which they will be) and whether your future pension accruals will be better, the same or worse.

There is no obligation (except where you have been working for the public sector and you are transferred to the private sector) to continue the same level of pension rights. Indeed, if you read the small print, the employer has the right to stop or reduce future pension rights at any time, to avoid him going bankrupt. You cannot normally regard it as grounds for unfair dismissal or redundancy just because the pension rights are changed for the future.

86 Trustee: Do you really want to be one?: pros and cons

There are some horror stories written about trustees, about the liabilities they are subject to and the penalties that may be imposed on them. But after the Pensions Act 1995 the law now encourages employees to volunteer to be a trustee, and if you have the opportunity, you should seriously consider it. You could do a very great deal of good – and the risks are in reality minuscule, provided you check one or two things.

Table 30   What to check before agreeing to be a trustee

☐ Have I been given a full set of papers, including trust deed and rules, accounts, actuarial reports, investment reports and trustee reports?

☐ Is there any litigation in progress?

☐ Is there any insurance to cover me against liability?

☐ Is there a power to resign in the Deed?

☐ Have there been any investigations by the authorities (Inland Revenue, OPRA)?

☐ Do I get on with the other trustees?

☐ Have we got all the advisers in place?

Who can be a trustee?

There are very few restrictions on who can be a trustee, but the law now requires, in company schemes, that employees are offered the right to elect up to a third of the trustee board. There is no obligation on employees to do so; if they cannot be bothered or are happy with the position as it is, then there will be no employee-nominated trustees (actually called member-nominated trustees).

You could be invited to be a trustee either by the employer or by the existing trustees inviting you to join them, or by being elected by your co-members in an election.

If I am a member trustee

The rules for member trustees are the same as for all trustees, with just the following small differences:

- they are not normally more than a third of the board

- you must be in office normally for at least three years and not more than six (you can always resign, of course)

- you are entitled (like any employee-trustees) to time off during work (i.e. with pay) for trustee training and to carry out your trustee duties.

The rules that require the scheme members to have the choice of member trustees are all schemes with employee members:

- schemes with 100 or more members must offer one-third of the seats, with a minimum of two member-trustees

- smaller schemes must offer at least one seat.

The employer can offer different arrangements to those laid down in the law, but must write to all employees saying what is proposed. If 10% of the workforce object, the question must be put to the workforce in a vote.

Penalties and liabilities

In theory there are over 200 criminal and nearly-criminal offences which make you liable as a trustee following the 1995 Pensions Act. So is the risk worth it? In practice there are two areas of liability.

- First, civil liability, i.e. any member, for example, could sue you if he or she was aggrieved by a decision you made, or you presided over a pension scheme that lost a lot of its money.

- Second, criminal liability, i.e. you break the law and have to pay a fine, or at the worst go to prison.

Both these possibilities are extremely remote (unless you actually steal the money).

- The Deed (i.e. the governing document) usually exempts you from liability, and the judges have recently looked at such provisions and found them very sensible for most trustees.

- The Deed usually contains an 'indemnity' from the employer, i.e. a promise that if anything happens, he will pick up the tab. This is a useful promise, but only good while the employer stays in business.

- The court will usually excuse you even so, if it feels it would be fair and reasonable to do so, and they are usually sympathetic to employee trustees.

- Sensible trustees arrange insurance against being sued or complained about, or become members of an association like the Occupational Pensions Defence Union (see page 266) which acts like a protection club for trustees. The point about it in particular is that not only does it provide cover like many insurance companies but also it manages claims (to try and save money) and protects you once you have left the scheme, perhaps because of retirement. It is the liability in retirement that causes most trustees grief, because it is then that the normal protections built into the trust document no longer apply.

In real life, therefore, provided you behave reasonably sensibly, there is nothing to worry about.

Duties

If you become a trustee, the duties should not occupy a great deal of time, since most of the day-to-day management is carried out by people the trustees hire to do the work for them, including:

- Administrators, to collect the contributions, pay the benefits and maintain the records. Very often this is the employer itself, but can be an insurance broker, pensions consultant, insurance company or specialist administrator.

- Accountants, to produce annual accounts.

- Actuaries (not really needed in many money-purchase schemes) to check whether there is enough in the kitty, and who must report at least every three years or so.

- Lawyers, when there are any problems.

- Investment managers, to invest the contributions and growth on the fund.

In the case of each of them their duties must be set out in writing, and in most cases your main duty is to keep an eye on them to check they are doing their job properly, and, if not, replace them.

You also normally have the following tasks:

- Meeting from time to time, to check how things are going. In a small scheme twice a year is enough, in the very largest schemes you might meet once a month.

- Checking that the trustees' records are properly kept (minutes have to be kept in a certain way, notices of meeting have to be given in a certain way in some cases).

- Deciding who should get death benefits after a member dies (using your discretion) after looking at letters written by members before they die.

- Exploring in some cases whether benefits might be improved if there is sufficient money available and the employer consents.

- Being trained, which is not a legal requirement but a sensible thing to do.

Table 31   Regulatory checklist for trustees

☐ Keep separate bank accounts for trustee money

☐ Make sure the employer pays any money he gets (for example, from an insurance company to pay benefits) in a separate bank account if he holds on to it for more than two days

☐ Make sure there is a contract with all advisers, investment managers and anyone who holds cash who is not a bank

☐ Keep minutes of meetings

☐ Produce accounts and trustees' report within seven months of year-end

☐ Ensure the administrator produces annual benefit statements

☐ Allow members to have copies of documents (e.g. deeds, rules, transfer values, etc.)

☐ Tell OPRA if the contributions are not paid on time

☐ Tell members before they hand money back to the employer

☐ Hire advisers (in writing)

☐ Get someone to prepare a statement of investment principles, to show what their objective is when investing and why

☐ Review all the documents from time to time

☐ Don't invest back in the employer (with some exceptions)

☐ Make sure there is enough money in the scheme to meet the liabilities

☐ (eventually) Keep a Schedule of Contributions, i.e. how much money the employer and employees are going to contribute over the next five years

Many of these will be done by your advisers rather than you.

You also need to make sure that there is a simple dispute resolution system; this will normally be organised by your advisers.

Things to watch

It can be a very fulfilling role to be a trustee. You are not there of course to negotiate on behalf of members or employees (that is part of the wage negotiating process) nor to push any particular or social objectives (it is not your money you are playing with).

But you are allowed to be both a trustee and take a benefit under the scheme (unlike most other kinds of trusts like charities).

It is useful to check that the documents are understandable and up to date. And that the members are aware of the benefits of joining the scheme, including the low costs and high benefits. If you do not market the scheme, probably no one else will.

87 Unconventional relationships

Same-sex relationships

Until very recently, same-sex relationships were not recognised by either employers or indeed the Inland Revenue. More recently there has been increasing sympathy for such situations; in the United States, for example, a well-known software company several years ago provided full benefits for same-sex partners.

That situation is still rare here, but a relaxation some years ago by the Inland Revenue allowed same-sex partners to be considered 'dependants' even if not financially dependent, and this relaxation is now used to provide benefits if the trustees wish it. It is still up to the trustees and employer how this relaxation is applied, so nothing is guaranteed; it is at their discretion (usually).

Polygamous relationships

Polygamous relationships are recognised in the UK. The position of pensions is however a little confused.

- The state pension is payable in full to the first spouse, but

- the private pension can be paid divided between several spouses if the contract says so or if the trustees agree.

Cohabitation

Cohabitation is no longer a rarity. More and more of us are living together in heterosexual relationships without getting married. But the law does not yet fully recognise such relationships, and cohabitees have uncertain expectations under their partner's pension arrangements.

A wife, for example, will automatically receive a Widow's Pension on the death of her husband, if that is what the scheme provides. But an unmarried partner will receive nothing automatically, and will have to prove dependency if she wishes to receive either a lump sum or a dependant's pension.

This situation is unlikely to change for some time.

See also EQUAL TREATMENT (page 133); GIRLFRIENDS AND OTHERS (page 141)

88 Unfair dismissal

See REDUNDANCY AND UNFAIR DISMISSAL (page 155)

89 Whistle-blowing

It was thought that one of the reasons that Mr Maxwell was able to dabble in the pension funds several years ago was because none of the advisers or regulators exchanged information with one another. The Pensions Act 1995 makes it compulsory for actuaries and auditors to tell the Regulator if there is a breach of the rules (and the Regulator can then investigate and decide what to do) and gives power to anyone else to write as well.

People who tell regulators have had an unhappy history in

the past; if you are an employee you might feel that you are putting your job at risk if you tell, for example, on your employer – and you would be right. The newspapers are full of stories of people who have told the authorities of a breach of the law and have found that not only have they lost their job but have found it all but impossible to get another one.

If you do find something that is not right, see if you can sort it out directly. If not, go and see one of the advisers who might be able to fix it, and who will be under a duty in many cases to sort it out themselves. You need to be very brave and sure of your ground before informing OPRA, and in such a case you might find it helpful first to get in touch with an organisation that specialises in helping people in your position (Public Concern at Work etc.). If you are a member of OPDU, you should ring their helpdesk.

90 Winding-up

See CLOSURE OF MY SCHEME (page 113)

SECTION

E

Higher Earners

An outline of the position affecting higher earners (if you are earning around £50,000 a year or more) is set out in Section A. This section explores some of the practical solutions to providing pensions for old age to higher earners.

91 Friendly societies: Shall I start my own?

At one time friendly societies were all the rage; if you and at least six others got together you could form your own mini-insurance company and cut the expenses and be free of the normal investment restrictions. The documentation is fairly complex and needs to be approved not only by the Inland Revenue but also by the Registrar of Friendly Societies, but apart from filing the annual returns the running of a friendly society is reasonably straightforward.

Large partnerships still continue to run these societies, which issued personal pension plans to their members (i.e. you and your partners) but for complex regulatory reasons most are now being converted into SIPPs.

92 Income drawdown: Should I defer buying an annuity?

Recent years have seen annuities offered by insurance companies at lower than normal rates. The reason is that interest rates have been very low, and annuity rates reflect those interest rates. The problem was that once you had retired you had to use the money in your personal pension to buy an annuity (i.e. an annual payment until death) at the retirement date, whatever the annuity rates at that time. This left you at the mercy of the stock markets and interest rates at the time you retire, and was unfair to some and beneficial to others.

The rules were therefore changed by the Inland Revenue some years ago to allow you not to have to buy at annuity at just the worst time and, in a way, run your own annuity.

The rules are a little complex, and you need the help of an adviser or insurance company to work out just what it means for you, but, in brief, you do not buy an annuity at retirement but instead elect to draw down some of the assets in your plan as a kind of mock-annuity. In order to avoid your spending more than you should in the early years and leaving nothing left for your later years, there are some rules (of course).

- The maximum you can take is 100% of a notional annuity calculated using figures provided by the Government Actuary, so you cannot take more in theory than you would have had from an insurance company if you had bought a normal annuity. This is calculated using what the yield is on gilt-edged securities (UK government bonds) and if this changes (as it does), the annuity will change.

- The minimum you can take is 35% of that maximum, although you can change the amount during the year, provided over the year the limits of 35% and 100% are not broken.

- During the withdrawal period, you cannot change providers, unless you then buy an annuity, although if your plan is a SIPP, you have a wider choice of switching (in some cases).

- If you die once you have started withdrawing from your fund, the balance of the assets is paid to your estate or to the scheme trustees, less tax charged at 35%.

- Alternatively, if you die, any dependant you have nominated (say, your spouse) can continue to draw a pension until you would have reached 75, or buy an annuity in the conventional way.

- If you want to take the cash tax-free from the fund, you must draw down some of the assets as a pension at the same time (and therefore pay tax at income tax rates on it). Most of these rules as designed less to help you than to ensure the Revenue gets its money on tax that it didn't get when you paid it in. So if you need some tax-free cash, you will also have to have some taxed pension.

- You cannot pay money into the pension plan once you have started to take benefits from it, although if you have other plans, you can pay into them (which also works if you have segmented plans, see above). It would be odd if you wanted to do so, however.

There are risks in using the income drawdown facility. The upside if you are not a healthy individual is that you do not have to enter into the gambling contract with the insurer, knowing that the insurer will probably win. If you die soon after buying the annuity, you will have got a lousy deal. On the other hand if you have a lot to live for (and people with pensions tend to live longer than those without, although whether this is cause and effect is not known), you in theory might be able to get better value. Even here, many people remain convinced that merely by leaving the money invested in gilts they can get a better pension than buying an annuity – and leave the capital preserved (even after tax) for the next generation. In many cases this is true; just why annuity rates are usually so unattractive is a mystery reserved to insurance company actuaries. Much is to do with insurance company overheads and expenses which can be considerable.

Using the income drawdown facility now offered by most personal pensions needs some expert technical advice, which is not always available. You need to review the position every three years, pay an adviser perhaps every year or at least every three years, and take a gamble on how your investments will perform and whether annuity rates will rise or fall. The costs involved and the risks exposed to are such that it is an option only where there is at least, say, £100,000 in the fund (and some would say £200,000).

If you use the facility, you need (or your adviser needs) to balance the assets in your fund between equities (shares) which offer the prospect of real returns and gilts (government bonds) which offer greater security and lower volatility of value. Some advisers may be skilled enough to try to match your life expectancy with appropriate dated gilts, but doing this for an individual rather than a group is tricky and often impossible.

If the stock market increases in value, income drawdown is usually better value than buying an annuity because the growth is kept by you rather than the insurer – and you do not have to bear the insurer's overheads. You do have management costs of your own, however.

93 Phased retirement: Do I have to take my pension all at once?

In most personal pension plans (this section does not apply to occupational schemes or SSASs) you must state the normal retirement age, which can be anything these days from 50 to 75. However, you may not need all that income immediately on retirement (you may be continuing part-time in some job, for example) and to take the whole pension may be inappropriate.

Most personal pension plans are therefore divided into mini-plans, some or all of which you can decide to retire under at different dates. In each mini-plan you decide when to retire and then take, say, the 25% of the assets in tax-free cash, and the balance as an annuity or pension. You must take any pension left by 75. You do not of course have to take the cash; you can use the whole of the money as pension.

For most people this option is a little sophisticated and messy, but where the potential pension is a substantial one it is worth considering, which is why it is placed in the higher income section of this book. If your income is modest, this arrangement is still possible but may not be worth the administrative overheads. But where annuity rates are low (as some feel they are at present) it is useful not to have to buy the full annuity at the outset, and wait until perhaps rates improve.

If you die before 75, the assets of the fund that is left are returned to your dependants and, if properly arranged, should be free of inheritance tax.

94 Small self-administered schemes (SSASs)

SSASs (small self-administered schemes) have been around now for about 25 years. They were first permitted in 1973 by a Finance Act which allowed company directors to be trustees of their own pension scheme, and in particular to pay fees instead of having commission deducted from their contributions, and to have a say in where their investments were made. In particular, they could lend money back to the company, to reduce a company's cash-flow problems when funding for pensions, and they could, for example, buy property from the company and rent it back, which meant that money could be released from the company to provide for pensions without having to lose control of the assets of the company.

For these reasons and many others SSASs became very popular amongst smaller companies, especially when tax rates were very much higher than today, because they offered highly tax-efficient pensions provision. Today, when tax rates are lower, and are unlikely to rise much, SSASs offer less attractive tax-planning, especially since the highest rates of tax are more bearable, and there is little difference between capital gains and the higher rates of personal taxation. But simply as a pensions vehicle, SSASs are administratively efficient, offer much lower overheads, and grant a facility of investment freedom which is very attractive. In addition there are many citizens (perhaps including you) who are uncomfortable about handing large sums over to insurers, who for all their remarkable qualities have not always been blessed with low-cost overheads, rapid response customer care and high-return investment management. While many insurers offer perfectly sensible SSASs themselves (sometimes known as 'hybrid' SASSs), the pure SSAS has nothing to do with an insurer; indeed, that is its main point.

Finding someone to help you set it up can be a bit of a problem. You can get a list of the main operators from the Association of Pensioneer Trustees (pensioneer spelt with three 'e's) which advise on SASSs; and several insurance companies also offer a service, which they find it difficult to make a living out of but do it so as not to lose touch with you.

You will (should) normally pay a fee for setting it up (the point about an SSAS is that expenses are transparent, rather than hidden) and you will need someone to help you draft the documents, obtain revenue approval, continue to monitor the scheme regularly and comply with the law. Once you have got one, you can monitor the growth of the funds, their investment and management with relative ease, save a great deal of money, and be astonished at how quickly the funds grow.

Table 32   What to watch for in an SSAS

- How much does it cost to set up?
- If the costs are based on funds under management, what are the costs over the next ten years expected to be?
- Are you a pensioneer trustee?
- Can I see the Pension Scheme Office authorisation?
- What are the expected annual and triennial running costs?
- Can I invest wherever I like, or am I tied to insurance policies?
- Is the money pooled with other people's or are there separate pots?
- Is the actuary a consulting actuary or an insurance actuary?

To establish an SSAS, you usually need:

- an actuary, to work out how much you can put in

- a lawyer to arrange the documentation and ensure you comply with the regulations.

You might also need an investment adviser if you do not want to manage the money yourself. There is no shortage of any of these; finding the right one can be difficult (see GETTING ADVICE, page 40).

Trustees

It is usual that all the members of an SSAS (including you) are also the trustees; that allows you to direct the investments if you wish and be in control of your retirement destiny. In addition, however, the Revenue insists that you appoint an additional trustee, approved by them, and known in the trade as a 'pensioneer trustee', to make sure that you comply with the Revenue rules and do not escape to the Bahamas or other

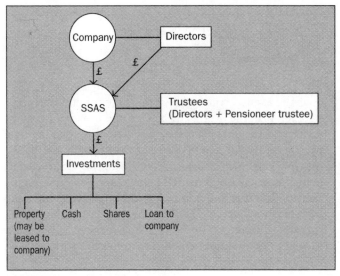

Figure 15   How an SSAS works

sensible clime with the tax-free money. Often your actuary
or lawyer will be authorised to be such a trustee, or you may
find a special one. If you are a trustee of the scheme (as you
ought to be), many of the normal trustee requirements of the
Pensions Act 1995 do not apply, because really you are trustee
of your own money, rather than other people's.

Investments

You can invest the money, within limits, wherever you wish.
You can, as most do, stay conventional: Marks & Spencer
shares, building society and bank accounts, government bonds
(gilts). You could be slightly more adventurous and buy
property (quite a common investment for SSASs) and rent it
back to the company. You can invest overseas as much as you
like. You cannot, however, invest in:

- shares in your own company over certain limits

- loans to your company over certain limits

- residential property (including, or rather, more especially,
  holiday homes)

- tangible assets, i.e. things you can touch (and remove or enjoy) such as racehorses or paintings.

There are downsides to SSASs.

- The cost can be significant (though usually much less than a wholly insured scheme). Assuming contributions of, say, £10,000 p.a., the overheads by way of a triennial fee to an actuary, occasional legal fees and annual accounting and pensioneer trustee fees might be around £1,000 p.a. To set that in context the hidden costs of a wholly insured scheme might be, say, £2,500 p.a. Of course, the more you put in, the less the costs are, relatively, and by the time the fund has grown to, say, £100,000 after five years, the cost is running at about 1% of funds under management, which is pretty low by most standards. Investment management fees are on top (say, 0.5% p.a.).

- If you get divorced, the value of the pension fund is easier to identify than with an insured scheme, or no scheme at all. You will need to make sure, if a divorce is in the air, and you attempt to minimise your liability, that the investments are in illiquid assets such as property, where the value can be minimised.

- At the end of the day you must (almost always) buy an annuity. While there are ways to defer buying an annuity, a stage comes where it must be acquired. An annuity is a gamble with an insurance company, and you are bound to lose it. But that is the price you pay for the fiscally neutral treatment you have enjoyed until that date, so don't be too greedy.

A small self-administered scheme is a standard form of pension provision if you have your own company. You might feel that your shareholding in your company is a pension in itself, and the provision of a pension is something for the wimps. But a pension scheme can assist in cash flow management and provide security against the possibility, however remote, that the shares could be worth a lot less than thought.

So setting up a scheme may have its advantages:

- Where contributions are significant (say, over £5,000 p.a.) the charges applying to an SSAS are usually much less than those applying to a pure insured scheme, such as a company pension for a director (sometimes known as an executive plan).

- The scheme allows the funds in the scheme to be invested in almost anything (including property).

- The scheme can be 'geared', i.e. it can borrow money to help buy investments, which in turn can ensure higher funds can be paid in.

- The trustees can (almost certainly will) include you, so that you can keep track of what is going on (or delegate it, if you prefer).

- You can pool the investments with your co-directors (so as to buy a property, for example), or invest separately to keep your assets separate from the others.

- You have control over the direction of management of the scheme, especially in take-over or merger arrangements.

- Contributions from the company and by you can be greater than contributions to personal pension or money-purchase schemes, and pensions therefore higher, although there are limits on how much you can put in.

Restrictions on investments

There are restrictions on investments which an SSAS can make, but they are relatively few. In particular, an SSAS can:

- make loans to the company and/or its subsidiaries (but not you or anyone connected with you)

- buy property from the company (but not from you or anyone connected with you)

- buy your company's shares.

SSASs have specific exemption from all sorts of controls that apply to conventional schemes, such as the member-trustee rules and the self-investment rules, provided:

- all members of the scheme are trustees and the scheme requires written consent of all members to any self-investment

- the trust deed requires trustees' decisions on investment policy to be unanimous

- all members are party to investment decisions.

There are, however, limits to the investments such a scheme can make, and certain other controls imposed, in order to avoid double tax relief arising.

LOANS

The SSAS can lend money back to the company, provided:

- The loan does not exceed 50% of the scheme's total assets (in the first two years, 25% of the total assets excluding transfers received from other schemes).

- There must be no regular pattern of lending back to the company part or all of the employer's regular contributions.

- The loan must be on commercial terms at a realistic rate of interest. The default rate is 3% over Base Rate unless evidence is shown to the contrary. Interest must be charged and paid, and there must be a loan agreement which states amongst other things what would happen if there is a breach of the agreement.

- The loan must be used for a genuine commercial purpose, e.g. for capital spending and not, for instance, to keep the business afloat.

- Unsecured loans must be short-term; secured loans can be longer term.

- The loan must be fixed term; successive 364-day loans (to enable the interest to be paid without deduction of tax) are not permitted.

- Loans to scheme members and their family are forbidden.

But even with these (often somewhat petty) restrictions, the facilities can be attractive.

PROPERTY

You can use the scheme to buy commercial property from the company, thus freeing up cash reserves, but if so:

- It must be at current market value supported by an independent valuation.

- The rental income must show a reasonable yield (say 8–10% p.a.), supported by the advice of an independent valuer.

- Investments in residential property are forbidden except in special circumstances (e.g. where it is occupied by an arm's-length employee such as a caretaker, or as a pure investment). This is to avoid present enjoyment of an investment on which tax relief has been given, so that holiday homes are out.

- There must be a plan to solve the liquidity problem so that when benefits fall to be paid there is sufficient cash to pay the pensions and other benefits, and the investments are not all locked up in illiquid property. Usually this is done by a simple cash flow projection taking account of rental income and future contributions.

- There should be some alternative investments, so as to protect against unexpected death benefit claims and having to sell the property at a bad time.

- Short-term borrowing to finance the purchase is fine (if permitted by the deed), and is attractive in many cases because:
  - the company contributions to the scheme (to buy the property) receive tax relief
  - the rent paid by the company to the scheme is an expense of the company for tax relief
  - the rent grows tax free in the scheme
  - when or if the property is sold any capital gain is realised tax free in the scheme.

COMPANY SHARES

Although it looks good in theory for a pension scheme to buy shares in the company, in practice it is not common. Although it might be useful in theory as a protection against an unwelcome take-over, this is less a problem in small private companies. And on the other hand most private companies have a modest or negligible dividend policy while the Revenue (paradoxically in the light of changes to Advance Corporation Tax in 1997 designed to reduce dividends in public companies) insist on a dividend policy. Before buying shares the scheme should:

- receive clearance from the Revenue (so there is no charge to income tax)

- check that there is a genuine commercial reason for it and not just to avoid tax

- check that the shareholding is taken into account when looking at the total interaction between the company and the scheme (including loans)

- check that the shareholding is proportionate; investing more than 25% of the fund in company shares may raise an eyebrow with the Revenue

- check the fund should not own more than 30% of the company

- note that the shares may have to be sold to pay pensions at some time, and this may be tricky (because only a few people are ready, willing and able to buy shares in a private company).

WORKS OF ART, CARS, ETC.

These are called 'pride in possession' investments, and because you would be enjoying not only the tax relief but also the pleasure of looking at them (and might be tempted to use them), they are forbidden as an asset of your scheme.

BORROWINGS

The scheme can borrow not more than three times the employer's annual contributions to the scheme and employee's contributions (excluding Additional Voluntary Contributions) and 45% of the scheme investments. There is a technical definition of 'ordinary annual contributions'.

Special controls

Because of the special advantages of an SSAS and the perceived opportunity for abuse (disappearing off to Spain without paying tax on the pension), there are special controls which do not apply to small schemes that invest only in insurance policies or larger schemes.

- There must be a 'pensioneer trustee' (spelled like that) who is a professional pensions person who will whistle-blow to the Revenue if any of the rules are broken. These special trustees are approved by the Inland Revenue and behave just like other trustees in other respects. The provision of a pensioneer trustee service is usually bundled in with whoever establishes the scheme for you. You can fire him but if you do, you must put another one in within a couple of months – and tell the Revenue within a month.

- There must (like other pension schemes) be actuarial reports every three years or so, if it is a final salary scheme at least, **and** (unlike other pension schemes) an investment report every three years **and** an undertaking by the trustees that the scheme does not break the Revenue rules.

- If there are not sufficient assets in the fund, any death-in-service benefits must be insured.

- The annuities bought by schemes when a member retires can be paid by the fund direct rather than bought from an insurer – but such an annuity must be bought when the member reaches 75.

- You must tell the Revenue of certain transactions, including loans to employers, purchase or sale of land, purchase or sale of shares in unquoted companies and purchase or sale of property from the employer, all within three months.

Is it worth my setting up an SSAS?

Setting up an SSAS is nowadays quite straightforward. Many insurance companies sell SSASs (known as 'hybrids', because they are not pure SSASs) and waive the establishment and management fees provided you invest a minimum amount with them in their funds.

A pure SSAS normally uses a series of advisers (perhaps bundled with one firm) including:

- a lawyer to get approval of the scheme from the Inland Revenue and draft the documents, and

- actuary to give advice on how much to put in, how to build up the scheme, and to certify to the Inland Revenue that not too much has been put in (he needs to repeat a valuation at least every three years)

- a pensioneer trustee as an Inland Revenue watchdog (who could be one of the above)

- an investment manager unless you do it yourself, and

- an administrator (again often the actuary) who keeps the records of contributions, bank accounts, Revenue returns and tax reclaims.

Although it sounds quite intimidating, in fact most of the professionals just get on with it. Costs vary enormously, depending on the amount of work involved (in other words, whether you are a difficult and active investor or a passive investor) but you might need to budget around, say, £2,500 p.a. set-up costs and about £1,000 a year on average maintenance costs. As the fund grows (and these funds grow dramatically), the costs diminish markedly and are usually much less than insurance company overheads, whose costs reflect the price of doing business with many smaller contributions.

The pros and cons

The benefits of SSASs are manifest:

- the opportunity to finance (through self-investment) the company through purchase of company assets, especially property

- the ability to put in more than you could in a personal pension

Table 33	SSASs: How much can I put in? Treating personal and company contributions as one					
	Executive pension plan		Small self-administered schemes		Personal pensions	
Entry age	Old	New	Old	New	Age	Max. Contr.
30	111%	33%	119%	33%	30	17.5%
35	120%	42%	125%	42%	36	20.0%
40	129%	55%	135%	55%	46	25.0%
45	147%	76%	152%	76%	51	30.0%
50	186%	118%	190%	118%	56	35.0%
55	310%	243%	213%	243%	61	40.0%

'Old' equates to the maximum contributions to a scheme set up before June 1996. 'New' refers to all schemes set up after June 1996. The limit applies to all schemes, regardless of when they were set up after 1 June 2001 .

Source: Churchill Pension Consultants, *Financial Adviser*, 25 September 1997

- the opportunity to finance the company by providing loans to the company of up to 50% of the value of the fund

- the opportunity to enhance investment returns where special opportunities emerge for investments, such as property developments

- the reduction in administration and management costs, compared with pure insurance company arrangements, whose charges have to reflect the costs of doing business with much smaller arrangements

- the opportunity to direct investments, including direct investment in shares or overseas shares

- the ability to delay having to buy an annuity

- the ability to introduce new members to use up any surplus provision without having to pay tax.

But there are downsides too ...

- there are costs (high where small contributions are involved) in paying professional advisers

- it is distracting (sometimes) for management to engage in managing a pension fund

- there are risks (manageable) in being a trustee

- investments can be more risky as well as higher reward

- transfer of assets to a pension fund from the company makes it harder for the company to raise loans outside

- establishment of an SSAS crystallises the value of pension rights which can be a problem where one of the directors is getting divorced

- there can be conflicts of interest if one of the directors leaves the company or wishes to pull out of the scheme and assets have to be realised to pay him out

- you need Inland Revenue permission before you transfer any arrangements out of the scheme

- you must tell the Inland Revenue if you buy property within 3 months.

There is no doubt that SSASs have proved almost standard

Table 34 How an SSAS buys property – I

Assume:
- Five directors
- Company owns property worth £100,000
- Five directors have saved up £115,000 in retirement annuity policies
- Company makes profits of £50,000
- Company pays corporation tax of £10,350
- Company pays £5,000 annual contribution into SASS

Company	£	Pension fund	£
Gross profits	50,000		
Less pension contribution of	5,000	Contribution from company of	5,000
Chargeable profit	45,000	Contribution from previous schemes	115,000
Corporation tax payable	10,350		
Net profit	34,650		
Cash flow	34,650		

Source: Commercial Union, Iain Oliver, *Financial Adviser*, 21 August 1997

Table 35 How an SSAS buys property – II

Assumptions as in Table 34:

But pension scheme buys factory/offices worth £100,000 from company, and rents back to company. No taxable gain on sale of property.

Company	£	Pension scheme	£
Gross profits	50,000		
Less pension contribution	5,000	Pension contribution	5,000
Less rent	10,000	Cash balance	15,000
Chargeable profits	35,000		
Corporation tax	8,050		
Net profit	26,950		
Property receipt	100,000	Property asset	100,000
Cash flow	126,950		

Advantages

- Property ownership in friendly hands (unlike sale and leaseback)
- Discharge of mortgage, if mortgaged
- Extra cash resources for company
- Property protected against company insolvency
- Pension rights for directors better protected against personal insolvency in company scheme

Disadvantages

- May have to pay CGT on sale of property
- Transaction costs (legals, stamp duty)
- Property may be worth less if company fails and no tenant

practice for family-controlled companies and, while they have their problems – in particular the complex Revenue controls and professional expenses – the benefits are generally perceived to have outweighed them. They are now part of the standard advice for most profitable companies and their director/shareholders.

95 SIPPs

SIPPs are a way of the self-employed also managing their retirement more efficiently. Usually available to those who can afford contributions of, say, £5,000 p.a., or who can put, say, £60,000 of transfer payments into the pot, it is a way of paying fees, rather than having commissions and expenses deducted. In other words, like an SSAS, it is a transparent way of providing for your old age.

You must use an external 'provider' (i.e. a bank, insurance company or other appropriate institution) to hold the money for you; but once you have handed it over, you can direct the investments, within limits, including the purchase of property.

The rules are somewhat different from an SSAS.

- You also pay fees, rather than have the usually higher commissions deducted from your contributions. That means you usually know how much you have in your retirement account, whether you leave it with that manager or transfer it elsewhere. There is no penalty for changing your mind, and the overheads anyway are usually significantly lower.

- You can direct the managers to invest at your direction, or appoint an expert fund manager, who can buy shares or government securities; or you can give it to an insurance company who will allow you to use their investment expertise, without charging for their distribution and selling skills. What you can invest in is set out on page 186.

- But you cannot invest in:
  - residential property at all
  - commercial property, unless it has had no connection with you or a member of your family in the past (unlike SSASs, where you are free to buy any property)
  - non-quoted securities.

All these rules are set out in a well-known (in the industry) Inland Revenue guidance note called Memo 101. Although it is several years old, it is still the major guidance on the subject. The main objective is to find someone who charges reasonable (though not rock-bottom) prices, is reasonably efficient in sending you annual statements, and can advise on the purchase of property, the one area where there is still a great deal of misunderstanding.

The purchase of property is much the most expensive form

of investment, and more expensive than buying a property through an SSAS, for example. The reason is that only a property can have a negative value, i.e. be worth less than zero (because, for example, of environmental clean-up bills imposed by a local authority). In an SSAS such a nightmare will not affect other SSASs; in a SIPP, which is essentially a grouped pension system, where you pool your investments with other subscribers (even though the accounts show your investment separately), a minus value could, unless carefully managed, infect other SIPP holders.

Finding a manager

You cannot simply set up a SIPP; you need a provider. There are several, but most are now branded versions using different charging techniques using one of three main providers. They are much of a muchness, and you should choose the adviser you feel most comfortable with to set one up for you. Filling out the form is not for the faint-hearted; you will find it difficult without professional help.

But, once in operation, you should find a SIPP a wonderfully cost-efficient and sensible way of providing for retirement, with added benefits on the investment management side.

Deferred annuities

One of the major problems of all pension systems is the confusion between savings and insurance. Everyone understands that if you gamble in a betting shop, say, a fiver on La Retraite to win, if it trails in last, you've lost your money. Similarly, if you gamble your life with an insurer, and you die the next day, you've lost; if you live for ever, you've won. But either way, you cannot normally have the return of your stake.

Even so, with the recent very high cost of annuities (compared with recent years) the requirement to buy an annuity can come as something of a shock. Often, £100,000 cash will only buy you a pension of, say, £5,000 p.a., depending on interest rates at the time. So the Inland Revenue relaxed the rule that made you use your money at retirement to buy an annuity and gave you until the age of 75 to buy the annuity.

Meanwhile, you could take some of the money in your retirement account or pension scheme on the drip. The Government Actuary has laid down some tables that make you take some of it every year until you do decide to buy an annuity; and if you die before you take the annuity, then tax has to be paid on the amount that's left before it goes to your spouse. But it is a welcome (though puzzling) relaxation, and one which is being widely adopted. It is not worth the effort, however, unless you have, say, £100,000 in your pension plan because the administrative expenses (including those of having to take advice every year) don't make it worthwhile under that amount.

One of the attractions of SIPPs is the ability to pay fees (rather than commission) and the ability to direct the contributions rather than be forced into a range of funds offered by an insurer. The other opportunity, to buy property, is also welcome to many people. However, until 1989 it was not possible (with some exceptions) for self-employed people to enjoy a similar range of benefits, and they were compelled to buy a pension from an insurer.

From 1989 the general rules were relaxed so that the self-employed could also be given the opportunity to invest themselves (hence 'self-invested personal pensions') and rules were introduced to avoid abuse of the system.

Such SIPPs are now increasingly popular, not only with wealthier people who can make substantial annual contributions (since those are now limited by the earnings cap to contributions on income up to £87,600 (1998/9) p.a.). These are, of course (as in so much in pensions matters), subject to quite complicated rules.

You can direct the investments you make into:

- stocks and shares (e.g. equities, gilts, debentures, etc.) quoted on the UK Stock Exchange, including securities traded on the Unlisted Securities Market

- stocks and shares traded on a recognised overseas stock exchange

- unit trusts and investment trusts

- insurance company managed funds and unit-linked funds

- deposit accounts

- commercial property.

What you cannot do is lend money from your scheme to yourself or anyone connected with it or you (even with security); and no loan from any source made to an individual who is a member of the scheme should in any way affect the return on investments representing that member's interest in the scheme. The reason is that the Inland Revenue are keen to see that schemes are not used to generate extra tax relief than that permitted under the legislation.

The rule against investment in residential property seems to be a movable feast; some observers have reported that the Inland Revenue permit such investment in, say, student hostel accommodation – provided it is clear that the policyholder cannot also enjoy occupying the property. There are also strict rules against buying property (or even shares) from a connected party (i.e. the policyholder and family) presumably because the Revenue smell a rat on values. Oddly, similar restrictions do not seem to apply to SSASs. The Inland Revenue issue standard rules for these schemes, which are quite complicated, but the investment rules seem to be settling down, although investment in milk quotas was uncertain as an investment for some years!

In practice you would almost certainly appoint an investment manager or adviser and these can be either an insurance company (which rather defeats the object of the exercise) or a bank or building society or unit trust manager – or, increasingly, independent financial advisers or stock-brokers.

However, one of the advantages of these schemes, besides the usual ones of transparent and limited charges, is the ability (as is available in SSASs) to buy property. And there is an unlimited ability to borrow to buy property, so the gearing effect can be significant (and necessary, since there are limits on the contributions). The borrowing limits that apply to SSASs have no place in SIPPs, although normal prudence would dictate that borrowing over 80% of value would be unwise, and should be accompanied by cash flow projections to ensure the lender has some chance of receiving his periodical payments.

96 Unapproved schemes: FURBSs and UURBSs

Background

If you earn over £87,600 p.a. (1998/9) you cannot (nor can your employer, if any) receive tax relief on pension contributions in relation to the income over that level. The level is called the 'earnings cap'.

So the question is: can anything be done to pension the excess salary? The answer is usually (if the will is there) an 'unapproved' scheme, i.e. a scheme that is not approved by the Inland Revenue. This means that the usual tax reliefs will not apply. Such schemes are used:

- where your employer wants to offer you more than the normal maximum of two-thirds of final salary

- where you have not completed 20 years' service, the normal minimum to qualify for a full two-thirds pension

- where you or your employer want to make pensionable income over £87,600.

Such arrangements are increasingly popular as more employees begin to earn over £87,600 a year or move to a job where the earnings cap applies if they were not caught by it before. They only apply to company arrangements; the self-employed or those with personal pensions can do nothing to improve their pension benefits over the £87,600 earnings cap.

At one time such schemes were rare; now about £500m a year is being paid into FURB schemes by employers, and the figures are increasing.

How it works

There are several forms of such arrangements; most boil down to two main kinds.

- A funded scheme (a FURBS – Funded Unapproved Retirement Benefits Scheme) where the employer pays money into a kitty, which means there is money there to pay some kind of benefit (but the tax relief does not apply), and

- An unfunded scheme (an UURBS – Unfunded Unapproved Retirement Benefits Scheme) where no money is put in, but benefits are paid when retirement age is reached. These are fine – but depend on the employer being in business when the benefits are paid, so the risk can be high.

Whatever system is adopted, it must provide 'retirement benefits', a technical term which includes most of the usual benefits (including retirement pensions and lump sums on retirement). It does not include accidental death and disability benefits or redundancy benefits.

Funded schemes

Funded schemes are normally better for you, because at least there is money there to ensure the employer's promise is met if later he should become insolvent. There are some major differences in comparison with a normal pension scheme, however.

- You have to pay tax on any contributions put into the scheme on your behalf at the time the contributions are made. And if you make contributions too, you do not get tax relief on those either, and for other reasons employee contributions are not usually permitted by the scheme rules.

- The assets in the scheme have to pay income tax and capital gains tax at the basic rate (23%); the special rate for trusts (34%) does not apply – and the trustees can use half the exemption from capital gains tax as well (around £3,200).

- You can (probably ought to) take all the benefits when you retire as a tax-free lump sum; any pension is taxable as PAYE and therefore it is very inefficient to take the benefits in pension form. If you want to, you can use the money to buy an annuity (called a purchased life annuity) to work as a pension, but again only the capital element of the payments is free of tax. It is probably better to live off the income invested.

- Contributions by your employer are usually deductible as a business expense unless the Revenue consider that they are not reasonable in the circumstances (e.g. large payments in respect of a director of a small company). This is not the place to discuss whether the contributions will be attacked by the Revenue; it is a matter for your employer (or your adviser, if you are the employer as well).

- From 1999 National Insurance has to be paid on the contributions.

- The scheme can also provide death-in-service benefits over the usual limits (i.e. 4 × £87,600), which can be tax-advantageous.

The bad news is that with a funded scheme you have to pay tax now on benefits you may not see for a long time (if ever). The good news is that you should be able to retire in comfort. Sometimes employers pay you enough so that you can afford to pay any tax charged, so that the tax is not a problem in practice.

At one time it was useful to set up the FURBS offshore (e.g. in Guernsey) where the assets could grow free of UK tax, but since November 1993 that is no longer attractive.

Benefits

Benefits can be taken in pension form, but double taxation would then occur as PAYE would have to be paid on the pension. It is more sensible to take the whole of the fund in cash.

Unfunded schemes

Unfunded schemes avoid the tax problems (i.e. that you have to pay tax on contributions that you do not see) – but you have to rely on the fact that the employer will stay in business and be able to meet his promises at the time you need him to. That is why they are very much less popular than FURBSs, but you might like to consider it in the absence of any other option. Your employer cannot usually get tax relief on the promise, only on the actual payment when it is made – although he should declare the promises in his annual accounts. There are therefore two main benefits:

- it is easier to top up a final salary promise; and

- there is no PAYE on contributions – because there aren't any.

When you get the benefits, you have to pay tax on either any lump sum or pension at the usual income tax rates.

SECTION

F

General

97 Complaints

See DISPUTES (page 194) and PENSIONS OMBUDSMAN (page 199)

98 Corporate governance

Your pension scheme, together with other pension schemes, controls around three-quarters of the UK stock market, as well as large chunks of shares in other stock markets around the world.

In the past if your investment manager did not approve of how the company was performing he or she could sell the shares and buy shares in something else. But this did little if nothing to control improper behaviour by the management of the company. Company management, with shareholders who never interfered, could pay themselves what they wanted, could engage in commercial activity that was suspect and treat the company as their own personal property. Private shareholders could not afford to take steps to object; institutional shareholders (like you) did not have the time or the interest.

But this has lead to extravagantly unacceptable actions by company management, and because in particular institutional shareholders have started to invest in indexed funds, where they have to have some or all the shares quoted in the stock market, the normal remedy of selling was not available.

The history of such cases as Maxwell, Polly Peck, BCCI and many others, including Hanson, indicated that in future pension funds and insurance companies would come under increasing pressure to do something about it. But until recently they did not have the resources or the skills to interfere – nor did they have the inclination, especially as they did not wish to be accused of interfering in the management of companies who could with some justification complain that pension funds have no idea how to run a company.

But over the last two or three years:

- the Cadbury Committee's report has been adopted by the Stock Exchange so that public quoted companies must now comply with the recommendations, must appoint non-executive directors, must appoint remuneration committees and must ensure that the share option scheme and other benefits reflect company performance

- the Greenbury Committee set out guidelines to ensure that salaries and other benefits which affect performance are disclosed to shareholders

- and the Hempel Committee (1997) set out some modifications.

All this has mostly in fact been driven by US investors whose corporate governance activity is several years ahead of our own. But it must be a welcome development that shareholders, even indirect shareholders like you, are having a useful impact on the proper control of management.

Corporate governance has some connections with other pressures towards ethical and social investments, and is increasingly imposing pressure on companies such as oil companies and tobacco companies to clean up their acts in environmental and health areas.

99   Disclosure

See INFORMATION AND DISCLOSURE (page 216)

100   Disputes

If you are a complaining kind of person, pensions is a dream world. Especially once you have retired, you can cause expense and misery to all sorts of people at very little expense or risk of expense to yourself by writing complaints all over the place. But you have to follow the procedure.

There are several routes depending on whether your complaint is about:

- a state pension
- a company pension, or
- a personal pension.

State pensions

Working out what you are entitled to from the basic pension or Additional Pension, especially if you were contracted out, needs mathematical skills which are denied to most of us.

But if you are aggrieved, you can complain about the calculations (or the way in which the Benefits Agency has exercised its discretion) by

- asking the Benefits Agency to review its decision or
- appealing to an independent tribunal.

You have to appeal within three months of receiving a decision and there is a form (NI246) which you have to use, on which you explain why you think the payments are incorrect, or that you are entitled to a benefit they refuse to pay.

You can attend the hearing in front of the Social Security Appeal Tribunal (a team of three independent people) and talk about your case; if you do not ask to appear, the decision will be made in your absence on the basis of the documents. If you do appear, you can take a friend or adviser or someone from the Citizens' Advice Bureau.

Occupational (company) pensions

If you have a complaint about your benefits or the administration of a company scheme you have several routes.

- Use the internal dispute procedure which every scheme by law must have; you have two bites at the cherry (see below).

- If that fails, complain to the Occupational Pensions Advisory Service.

- If that fails, complain to the Pensions Ombudsman. So far, no costs are involved, apart from your time (and maybe that of others). Then, it can get expensive ...

- If that fails, complain to the High Court.

- After that, try the Court of Appeal.

- You might get permission to appeal again to the House of Lords.

- At any stage in the proper courts, you might find your case gets referred to the European Court of Justice in Luxembourg (as happened with cases on equal treatment in pension schemes).

- You could also try a complaint to the European Commission on Human Rights, and if they give permission ...

- Pursue a case in the European Court of Human Rights (in Strasbourg).

- In some cases you can pursue a pension claim in an Industrial Tribunal.

- In any case where you feel the law is not being followed by your scheme, complain to the Occupational Pensions Regulatory Authority.

Internal dispute procedures

Internal dispute procedures must be organised by every occupational pension scheme by law.

- The procedure is in two stages (usually set out in your member's booklet or your annual benefit statement, which says who the complaints are to be made to):
  - a first complaint, usually made to the day-to-day administrator, perhaps a full-time pension scheme manager, or an external administrator. They have to give a decision within two months.

– a second complaint, made to all the trustees.

● Almost anyone can complain: if you are a member, a widow or widower, surviving dependant, even a prospective member, or you were one of these within the last six months. And you can make the complaint yourself, or ask someone to do it on your behalf.

● You have to set out in writing what your problem is (including your name, address, date of birth, National Insurance number), similar details of anyone acting on your behalf – and you have to sign the complaint.

● A decision must be sent to you (and your representative) in writing within two months, referring to any of the rules, the law and your right of appeal. You have the right to appeal within six months, using the second complaint process to the trustees.

● They also have to reply (usually) within two months and, as well as giving you reasons for their decision, remind you that if you are unhappy, you can go to the Occupational Pensions Advisory Service and the Pensions Ombudsman. If they cannot reply in time, they must explain why they need more time.

If there is a problem with all this, you can complain that the procedure is not being properly organised to the Occupational Pensions Regulatory Authority.

Occupational Pensions Advisory Service

The Occupational Pensions Advisory Service is a voluntary independent organisation, grant-aided (i.e. it gets its money from the DSS via OPRA). It is set up to help members of the public who have problems with company pension schemes or personal pension plans.

Around 28,000 people a year use the services of the Occupational Pensions Advisory Service (OPAS) – not surprising, since the service is free. Most of the advisers, who are not remunerated, are in full-time employment and are experienced in pensions matters. If you have a problem which the internal dispute resolution system has not resolved, OPAS will:

- explain your benefits if you do not understand what you have been told

- obtain information from your pension scheme or plan if you have not been able to obtain what you need

- try to make sure you receive the benefits you are entitled to.

But OPAS cannot help:

- if your problem is about your job (rather than your pension)

- if your problem is about social security (including state pensions)

- if you want advice on the best investments for pensions or on the best scheme to be in

- representatives of groups of scheme members – complaints can only be accepted from individuals

- if you want to try to change the rules of a pension arrangement or lobby for improvements

- if the Pensions Ombudsman has already investigated your complaint

- if you have already started legal proceedings.

If OPAS cannot help you, it is supposed to tell you what else you can do.

IN PRACTICE ...

Once you have complained to OPAS you will be given an adviser, an unpaid (by OPAS) pensions professional who acts independently in accordance with an OPAS Code of Practice. You should get in touch with them by ringing 0171 233 8080 (see ADDRESSES, page 256). When you write to them you have to explain your problem, and enclose copies of any relevant papers; alternatively you can contact your local Citizens' Advice Bureau (see local telephone directory) who will find you an adviser.

Pensions Ombudsman

The Pensions Ombudsman investigates and decides complaints and disputes concerning occupational schemes; he is independent and acts as an impartial adjudicator. He covers the United Kingdom (including Northern Ireland and the Isle of Man) and there are no charges for bringing complaints or disputes.

WHAT CAN YOU COMPLAIN TO HIM ABOUT?

The Pensions Ombudsman can investigate

- complaints of maladministration by anyone responsible for the management of occupational pension schemes. The complaint may be against those who are or have been trustees, managers, employers and administrators. Maladministration involves 'bias, neglect, inattention, delay, incompetence, ineptitude, perversity, turpitude, arbitrariness'. It is not enough that you merely disagree with a decision; you must have reason to believe that the decision was not properly made or implemented.

- disputes of fact or law concerning pension schemes with trustees or managers or employers (but not other administrators). They usually arise incidentally to a complaint of maladministration without needing a separate investigation.

WHAT CAN'T YOU COMPLAIN TO HIM ABOUT?

You cannot use him to complain about the following.

- A complaint which is already being dealt with by a court (including an industrial tribunal).

- A complaint or dispute about a state social security benefit (e.g. basic state pension).

- Non-compliance with the law (which applied after April 1997) on
  - the requirement for member-nominated trustees
  - the payment of surplus or excess assets to the employer

- restriction on employer-related investments
- requirement to appoint professional advisers
- requirement to keep books and records
- the minimum funding requirements and schedules of contributions
- the requirement for money-purchase schemes to keep schedules of payments.

All these need to be referred to the Occupational Pensions Regulatory Authority. The Pensions Ombudsman cannot make any finding of fact on whether or not there has been compliance with the requirements of the Pensions Act 1995 (i.e. the list above).

- Personal pensions, which is dealt with by the Personal Investment Authority (see below). A complaint or dispute about the administration of a personal pension is dealt with by the PIA Ombudsman if the matter is within his jurisdiction, and otherwise by the Pensions Ombudsman. It is not unknown for complainants to be shuttled back and forth, since they are both overworked and could do without more cases; persistence pays.

- A complaint already being dealt with by another ombudsman.

- Any complaint where you have not first exhausted your rights to have the matter sorted out by the internal dispute procedure in the pension scheme, and the trustees or managers have issued their notice of decision (unless it is a complaint against employers or administrators).

- At his discretion where you have not then approached the Occupational Pensions Advisory Service to try and sort it out first without a complaint.

WHO CAN COMPLAIN?

You can complain if you allege injustice (which means not only financial loss but also distress, delay or inconvenience) and

- you are a member of the scheme (including anyone claiming to be or to be entitled to be a member and anyone with pensionable service but who left the scheme before reaching retirement age)

- a widow, widower or surviving dependant of a deceased member of the scheme.

  If you have died, your complaint does not necessarily die with you; any complaint can be pursued on your behalf by your personal representative (and minors can use grown-ups).

You can without any allegation of injustice

- refer, if you are anyone mentioned just above who is eligible to complain, a dispute of fact or law to the Pensions Ombudsman

- complain, if you are also a trustee, about:
  - the employer's maladministration
  - the maladministration of trustees or managers of another scheme

- complain if you are an employer of a pension scheme and want to complain about the trustees or managers.

WHEN MUST YOU COMPLAIN?

A complaint is not like a cold; if you nurse it, it will get worse. You must write to the Ombudsman within three years of the act or omission that you are complaining about or disputing. If you did not know about the matter at the time, the three years runs from the time that you knew or ought to have known. The Pensions Ombudsman can extend the time limit where he thinks it reasonable to do so (and in particular will disregard time spent using the internal dispute procedure and with OPAS).

HOW DO I MAKE A COMPLAINT?

If the internal dispute resolution system doesn't work, and OPAS doesn't help you:

- check that the dispute comes within his jurisdiction.

- Write, explaining your complaint or dispute and saying what you think the people responsible for the management of your scheme should do to put matters right. There is a standard form available (just ring and they'll send it).

- Enclose with your complaint (copies of) all the relevant documents and correspondence, including any with your pension scheme or employer or administrator. The Ombudsman will not take telephone complaints.

- If it would help, use someone else to write for you (solicitor, accountant, trade union representative) and give them written authority for them to do so. You will have to be prepared to pay any professional fees yourself; they may not be recoverable.

- There is no need to send the correspondence with OPAS, provided you have written to them to say it is okay for them to release their papers to the Pensions Ombudsman. This is not difficult for them, they live in the same office block (though on a separate floor).

AFTER YOU MAKE THE COMPLAINT ...

Once you have made your complaint, the Pensions Ombudsman

- checks that your complaint can actually been handled by him (if he can't, he will explain in writing why not, and suggest other Ombdusmen or complaints procedures, while returning the papers).

- If he can take it on, and he thinks it right that he should do so, he will start an investigation, and may ask you for more information. If after all this, he then decides not to take it further, he will write and explain.

- If he proceeds, he will write to the people responsible for the management of the scheme with copies of the details of the complaint, explaining how far he is investigating and asking them to respond within a few weeks. If you and they settle the dispute (as happens), he will stop; otherwise, he continues the investigations until he has the information he needs to make a decision.

- If you are in a hurry, you need to be patient. First, there is a major backlog. Second, once he starts the process it can take several months:

    - to put the information together, including asking for pension scheme records, rules and administrative procedures, anyone else he thinks should produce information, and if there is difficulty in getting it, compelling them to do so
    - to invite the other side to put their case
    - to ask you to respond to it
    - to possibly organise a hearing (rare; almost all cases are dealt with by post)
    - to consider the case
    - to write a draft decision (called a 'determination')
    - to send it to everyone for their comments
    - to issue the final decision, with reasons to everyone involved.

- If you don't like the decision, it is only possible to appeal on a point of law, not a point of fact. Employers and trustees are uncomfortable about this, because he could make a mistake involving millions of pounds and there is no appeal. On the other hand it does reduce the expense of legal fees and the time involved. If you want to appeal on a point of law, you can do so to the High Court (in Scotland the Court of Session; in Northern Ireland, the Court of Appeal). Remember, the other side can also appeal, and that could involve you in paying not only your but also their legal costs.

- There is little confidentiality in the process; the Pensions Ombudsman may disclose details about you and the complaint or dispute (including copies of documents and correspondence) to anyone else involved in the dispute, or anyone he needs to consult. And the decision will be reported and published in due course.

101 Divorce

The question of what to do on divorce about the pensions has been a running sore for many years.

Divorce is one of the growth industries of the United Kingdom. The reasons are not certain, but probably include the growing financial independence of women (and who now have the power to leave an unsatisfactory marriage) and higher expectations, as well as lower peer pressure against divorce.

In any event, with around 180,000 divorces a year, the legal issues of who was to blame have now almost disappeared; the major issue in most divorces, after the welfare of the children, is the financial distribution. And the largest item in most people's finances, even taking into account the house, is the pension.

Because of the problem that pensions posed in divorce, there have been recent reforms, and more are proposed. In August 1996 the courts were given power to make awards against pension funds (both personal and occupational), directing that either lump sums could be awarded and/or periodical pension payments. The process is now known as 'earmarking'. The problem is that the pension payments cease on the death of the member (and the former spouse) or on the remarriage of the spouse. And lump sum payments have to be made even after death of the spouse. The discomfort of all parties in this reflects the oddity of a pension: it is not a conventional asset like a house or a bank account that lends itself to division; nor is it insurance which is spent as soon as it is bought.

In practice, therefore, most parties still seek to use offsetting, i.e. using spare assets to discharge pension liabilities. This unfortunately is not always possible if there are no spare assets around. This might be if you are, or are married to, a policeman, fireman or teacher, where income may be modest and pensions a disproportionate percentage of the family's assets. But offsetting has its problems too, and the greatest is that of valuing in present cash the future benefits, taking into account the different tax treatment and life expectancies.

Eventually the government has announced that a third option will be introduced, that of pension splitting or, more politically correctly nowadays, pensions sharing. This involves the spouse taking part or all of a cash equivalent transfer value on divorce (rather than taking their chances at retirement with an earmarking order).

The state benefits

You will get (if you are a woman – there is no sex equality here) a state pension based on your husband's record. You will get the higher of the pension based on your own record or his record from the date of the marriage to the date of divorce, or the beginning of when you started to work until the date of divorce. You will not get any of his Graduated or Additional Pension.

If the divorce took place before pension age and you paid contributions at the reduced (married women's) rate, you must start to pay the full rate.

If the divorce took place after pension age and you are receiving the married woman's pension, you can get a pension based on your husband's contribution record up to the year in which you reach pension age (not the date he reaches pension age).

REMARRIAGE

If you remarry before pension age, you lose the right to use your husband's contribution record. If you divorce a second time, you can only use the last husband's record. If you remarry after pension age, the pension in payment continues.

SEPARATION

If you are separated, you are still married once a husband starts to claim his Retirement Pension. You can claim the married women's pension (unless you qualify on your own record).

If you are under 60, your husband gets the dependant's increase only if he contributes to your maintenance, which he is not if you are separated.

COHABITATION

See GIRLFRIENDS AND OTHERS (page 141)

What do you want if you are the spouse?

It is not easy to try and decide what is best for you about the pension rights of your spouse, assuming he is the scheme member. You have three options.

- To accept cash in lieu of pension rights. Assuming the value of your partner's pension rights is valued at, say, £10,000, you would think you should get, say, £5,000, assuming you have been married a fair while. But remember, you are getting cash which you can spend now (and not a pension which you may have died before you get there), you are getting it tax-free (instead of a pension which would normally bear tax at a maximum at present of 40%) and it is being paid many years in advance. You might accept perhaps 30% or less of the nominal value in exchange for this deal; alternatively if your spouse cannot buy you out (perhaps because he does not have the free resources), you could go for ...

- ... a court order that you could receive part or all of any lump sum arising on his retirement (and directing him to retire at a certain age). The problem with such an order is that it survives your death or remarriage, so he may be less willing to agree it, but if he is likely to die (because he is overweight or engages in unnatural sexual practices) soon, then it might be a good idea to go for, for example, part or all of a death-in-service benefit. Of course, he may be made redundant in which case the cover would not be there, and it is not sure whether you would get a similar order on another scheme.

- An order that he pay some or all of any of his pension arising at retirement to you. That might be a very attractive offer; however, it will fail if he dies, or if you die, or if you get remarried. If these are in contemplation, using one of the other options may be preferable, but may not be on offer.

In due course the government has announced that a fourth option will be available.

- The court will have the right to 'split' or 'share' the pension at divorce. This means that you will be able to take some or all of any transfer value of your spouse's pension and either have it transferred into your name or transfer it into a separate policy in your name with another provider.

The problem of valuation

A major problem is deciding just how much your pension rights are worth. By law the spouse must put on the list of assets the value of his pension rights using a method called the 'cash equivalent transfer value' or CETV. This value is, in the case of a personal pension, the surrender value, i.e. the amount available if you took your ball away and gave it to someone else, or somewhat similar in the case of a personal pension. In the case of a money-purchase occupational scheme the value will not be very different.

In these cases the value will be much less (often very much less) than what it would cost you to buy a pension of equivalent value from another provider (for the reasons for this, see TRANSFERS, page 244).

The question then arises: Which is the better value and most appropriate for you and your spouse?

- the cash, but no pension (the cash will not be enough to buy you an equivalent pension, but it may be more useful to meet immediate bills)

- a periodical payments order against the pension when it comes into payment, with the risk that it will not be paid

- a lump sum order, which depends on the unlikely (in most cases) event of him dying before retirement with the same firm

- a split of the pension at divorce which will put some money into your pension scheme, but will usually be pretty modest (available from April 2000).

If you are married to a higher earner

The situation is slightly different if you are or were married to a higher earner, especially one who

- has his own company

- employed you in the company

- has a small self-administered scheme or similar equivalent

- has a surplus in the scheme or where other arrangements can be made so that giving you a share of the fund would not affect any other member of the scheme.

In such a case the court may be prepared (and the Revenue likewise) to declare you a member of the scheme and give you your own rights. Such arrangements are not common, but are increasing slightly as the courts become more familiar with the process. Because you normally need independent actuarial advice, and it requires negotiation with the Inland Revenue, it is normally not worth the expense unless substantial sums are involved.

Remember if you get an earmarking order (i.e. to pay you a pension when he reaches retirement age), that pension will not be paid unless you tell the insurance company or pension scheme trustees of your change of address when or if you move.

If you are the member

If it is your pension that is being discussed on a divorce, you should not despair. First, in the list of your assets the pension is required to be valued at its lowest value, that is, as mentioned above, the CETV. In practice the courts (if it gets that far) will usually try to award cash rather than a share of the pension, to avoid future complexity. The cash payment will usually be very much less than half the CETV. If you do not have the cash to pay off the pension claim, then an earmarking order may be unwelcome, especially if you are going through perhaps a second divorce or are contemplating remarriage. But such orders are proving rare in practice; only eight were made in the first year they were available. Finally, if and when pensions splitting comes in, giving up half (say) of your transfer value may not mean giving up half your pension rights if you are in a 'final salary' scheme and intend staying with your employer for a little while yet. And if you move overseas, you can take your pension with you, and any court orders will be difficult to enforce once you have gone.

Table 36 What to do about your pension on divorce

- Consider 'offsetting', 'earmarking' lump sums and 'earmarking' pensions as alternative options (or mix and match).

- Remember to keep the scheme authorities informed of your address if you move; if they can't find you they can't pay you.

- When planning, consider whether you are intending to remarry, and the state of health of you and your (former) spouse.

- Consider delaying proceedings until 'sharing' becomes an option in due course.

Can your scheme cope?

Remember, your scheme may not be up to speed on responding to requests for information: it will need to be able to provide more than one transfer value quotation a year, and provide a valuation (valuing member's pension and death benefits separately) on a non-standard basis. They will also need to be able to register court orders and have a process by which they need to respond to proposed court orders if they feel they cannot comply with them. Any benefit statement must also include details of accrued benefits valued, a statement as to whether or not any discretionary benefits have been taken into account, and an explanation if the cash equivalent has been reduced because the scheme is underfunded. There must also be a statement (if requested to do so) testifying what proportion of cash equivalent is in their opinion attributable to any pension which the spouse would or might become entitled to in the event of the member's death. The scheme can charge (reasonably) for all this.

If the member moves his benefits, the scheme must notify the new scheme of the existence of the court order and send it a copy of the order (within 14 days). And the former spouse must be told of the date the benefits have been transferred, that the benefits have been transferred, the name and address of the receiving scheme and confirmation that the order applies to the receiving scheme. Of course, if the receiving scheme is overseas, applying such an order may be a problem. And the receiving scheme must have a system to keep track of transfers-in which carry a court order.

The scheme also needs to monitor the existence of the former spouse and stop benefits if there is death or remarriage.

In practice such orders have proved, so far, to be rare. The reason for this is not clear, and it may be early days yet.

102 Doctors and dentists

For reasons which are now rather ancient, if you are a doctor or dentist, you are treated very tenderly in relation to pensions. Most doctors and dentists are members of the NHS Superannuation Scheme, which offers very attractive benefits at very modest cost. If you have the opportunity to join the NHS Scheme you should do so immediately.

While the earnings are earnings from employment (under Schedule E) you cannot use them also to pay earnings into a personal pension. You may of course also have private earnings (under Schedule D), and you can pay the usual contributions into a personal pension.

However, you can choose in many cases to be treated as self-employed, even though paid by the NHS. There is a special concession that allows you still to be a member of the NHS scheme (which again you should think carefully about before avoiding) but, strictly, you will not get tax relief on the contributions (about 6%). But the Revenue in fact allow you to get both tax relief on those contributions as well as contributions in relation to any other income you have to a personal pension – and you can pay contributions in relation to your NHS income as well (although then you will not get tax relief on the contributions to the NHS scheme). Only doctors and dentists have this concession which is obviously carefully guarded. The opportunity to be both in a company scheme and a personal pension scheme is somewhat rare (as is the opportunity to exceed normal Revenue limits on benefits denied to ordinary mortals) – and very valuable. It is also why you see so many healthy doctors on expensive golf courses round Britain.

103 Early retirement: state benefits

You might wish to stop working before the State Pension Age. It is possible that you could receive the full Basic Pension (when you get to that age) without having to make further NI contributions. If you are under 60 and seeking work it is sensible to register for the Jobseeker's Allowance so that you will get pension credits paid for you. If you are a man aged 60–64, you automatically receive credits even though you do not sign on as unemployed or receive another benefit, provided you are not self-employed or overseas for more than six months.

104 Europe

So far the impact of the European Union on pensions policy has been limited – but over the next few years it is likely to increase quite a lot. The reason is that EU social policy requires a level playing field in member states so as to avoid one country having an unfair advantage over another, as well as general moral imperatives requiring proper treatment of employees. The impact of the EU applies particularly in areas of equal treatment, financial affairs such as investment controls and tax, mobility of labour and employment protection.

The EU has had an impact on:

- **Equal treatment.** Since a famous (to pensions people) case called *Barber vs GRE* in 1990, it has been illegal in the UK to discriminate between men and women in pensions provision in company schemes; it is still legal, however, to discriminate where there are actuarial reasons to do so, such as the fact that women as a group live longer than men as a group (and are therefore more expensive to provide pensions for). But equal treatment must be given under EU law for both membership, and retirement ages, as well as benefits, although certain specific benefits can be sex-preferential (such as pensions coverage for maternity leave).

The impact of the law has been significant:

Later decisions in the European Court of Justice have extended the scope of the legislation, so that almost all UK

Table 37   Impact of changes in equal treatment

Proportion of pension schemes with equal retirement ages

1988	22%
1989	44%
1990	53%
1991	75%
1992	85%
1993	90%

Source: NAPF surveys

schemes now offer equal treatment, although there are certain question marks over the protection of part-timers and how far back claims can go (see EQUAL TREATMENT, page 133).

- **Mobility of labour**. There have been several attempts to improve the right of scheme members to move their rights if they move to jobs in different parts of the EU. If you move from, say, the UK to France, you may have problems moving your private pension rights. State pension rights are protected by EU legislation which has now been in force highly effectively for over 20 years. But there are still problems if you leave a scheme in Germany, for example, to join a UK scheme, because German law only requires pension schemes to protect your pension rights if you have worked with the company for at least 10 years. If you leave before then, you could lose all your pension rights. In due course, the EU may improve your rights if you transfer from scheme to scheme.

- **Free movement of capital and services**. For most, this is a bit esoteric. It will allow (if it ever happens) pension schemes to invest freely throughout Europe. Although the UK has very few restrictions, other countries prevent their pension schemes investing outside their own country. More importantly for all of us, in due course it may be that we can join a scheme (and receive tax relief) in any EU country, so that we could choose whichever tax system was the best – and simplest. If this happens, the UK Inland Revenue would have to improve its service in order to compete, for example, with Luxembourg.

- **Employment protection.** It was EU law in bankruptcy that persuaded the UK government to introduce a compensation fund for company pension schemes which now helps at least in cases of maladministration. Whether it should also apply when the employer goes bust without fraud is another question and has yet to be tested in the courts.

Eventually it is expected that you will be able to move your scheme membership and personal pension rights around Europe, just as at present you could (in theory at least) maintain your state pension arrangements even though you work in a succession of member states. And meanwhile, many thousands of people have already had their pension rights enhanced as a consequence of a series of decisions in the European Court of Justice.

EMU

The impact of a currency union is difficult at present to estimate; however, if interest rates in Britain fall to European levels, it could make annuity purchases (if you are in a personal pension or a money-purchase scheme) twice as expensive; in other words, your pension might be halved. On the other hand, inflation should be lower, and it may be that the assets of your pension scheme could double. No need to panic just yet, and by the time it is time to panic, there is nothing you can do about it.

105 Forfeiture and set-off

In company schemes there is sometimes a rule that says that if you do something very dreadful, your pension could be forfeited. These rules are particularly draconian in public sector schemes, especially the civil service, or police, firemen or teachers.

The rules sometimes say that if you steal from the employer, or commit an act of treachery or espionage, then your pension will disappear. This can be a very substantial additional penalty in addition, for example, to any loss of job and, in extreme cases, prison.

This problem was discussed by the Goode Report on Pensions Law Reform, and the Pensions Act 1995 which followed. It made it clear that from 1997 while pension funds could indeed continue to include such rules, they could only be enforced with an order from the court.

There is no experience yet with such court orders, and it is unlikely that they will be given lightly. The position is also somewhat unfair because there would be no right, if your pension was a personal one, for the employer to get at your personal pension if you owed him money or if you had committed a dreadful act against him; so he has an extra weapon to control you in such cases.

If you feel that you might be exposed to such a problem, it would be sensible to arrange to move your pension, using your right to transfer out of a company scheme, to a personal pension in your own name. It may not be quite such good value, but it would avoid the possibility of the employer clamping your pension as part of a general battle.

106 Illness: sickness and disability

The purpose of a retirement pension is to protect you against the costs of old age. The pension normally kicks in when you reach retirement age. But it may unhappily be that you are too ill to continue working, or have to take a break in your employment career to cope with an illness. The consequences are different depending on the nature of the pension.

State benefits

If you are too ill to work you will normally get

- credits towards your state pension

- Statutory Sick Pay for the first 28 weeks of illness, then you move onto

- Incapacity Benefit, which you get if you are incapable of all work.

When you get to State Pension Age the long-term Incapacity Benefit stops, and you will start to get whatever Basic and Additional Pension arises plus an age addition to the Incapacity Benefit (subject to earnings limits).

Some people decide to go abroad, where it is warmer, to ease an affliction. If you do so, the Incapacity Benefit may well be stopped, unless you stay within the European Union.

Private scheme arrangements

You will not automatically get an ill-health or disability pension from your company scheme (and will not from your personal pension). The scheme may not contain cover, and even if it does, it may not cover you, especially if you have previously had a record of ill-health and are a higher earner.

The extent of the cover should normally be set out in the member's booklet and other correspondence; in any event you will need to check with the scheme administrator, and in particular get a copy of the rules relating to ill-health benefits, which go into the matter in much greater detail than the member's booklet. If there is a doubt, it is the rules that prevail. It will also tell you how to make a claim.

Your employer may have made an arrangement with an insurance company outside the pension scheme to provide cover through what is known as a permanent health insurance scheme and it may be the insurer that decides whether you can claim, rather than your employer.

The rules of schemes vary considerably, but many only allow an ill-health pension to be paid if you are unable to do any job at all anywhere. If you are fit enough to do some other job, you may not qualify even though you have to stop your current employment because of ill-health. And the fact that your doctor certifies you not fit for work may not in itself be sufficient to qualify you for a pension on the grounds of ill-health. Most schemes will ask for a report from their own doctor rather than yours, even if you have a specialist, and may sometimes ask you to pay for it (where the rules allow). The reason is simple: ill-health schemes are extremely expensive, and the scope for abuse is wide. Certain local authorities in Wales often used to allow their senior officials to retire on an ill-health pension only to discover them working the next year in a neighbouring authority.

Furthermore, even if you gain a disability benefit from the DSS (see above), that in itself will not be enough to qualify you for a private ill-health pension; the scheme rules will prevail. This raises a common question: what happens if the scheme rules and the booklet differ? In practice, you can often choose the one that is most beneficial for you, but you will need advice first, perhaps from OPAS. Lastly, the rules often allow the trustees to exercise their discretion on whether or not to pay you; you can only challenge their discretion (if it is not in your favour) if you can show they have behaved unreasonably or dishonestly (perhaps they have not taken into account all the information you think they should have). If your employer has the discretion (rather than the trustees), you may need to show that if they have refused you, it is to save money rather than because you have a poor claim. And in all cases your employer and trustees have to comply with the Inland Revenue rules which are very tight on when ill-health pensions can be granted (you need to be pretty sick).

107 Information and disclosure

State benefits

State benefits are almost impossible to work out on your own; you need a computer and a vast collection of records, not only of your own career but also of your spouse.

Only the government can maintain such records, and they do. If you would like to know what your state retirement benefits are or are likely to be, you can (if you are under 64 years 8 months if a man and 59 years 8 months if a woman) get a forecast from the Benefits Agency (which runs this part of the social security system).

You can get a form B19 from the local office (in the phone book under 'Benefits Agency') which comes with its own envelope and send it to the Retirement Pension Forecasting Unit. The forecast will deal with your Basic State Pension, your Additional Pension and your Graduated Pension based on your contributions to date and tell you how much you have built up so far and (assuming you continue to pay National Insurance contributions) how much you will get at State Retirement Age – and gives advice on how to improve your benefits. You can also apply to find out what you would get if you are divorced or widowed on the earnings record of your (married) partner.

It also gives you forecast options in different situations, including:

- if you work on after retirement age

- if you retire before retirement age

- if you go overseas

- if you start paying the full rate after paying reduced rate (if a married woman)

- if you pay extra contributions to make up for missing ones

- what happens if you get divorced or married

- what happens if your annual earnings change.

Personal pensions

If you are in a personal pension, you are entitled to an annual statement of how much is in the scheme, who is managing it, and who to complain to if you have a problem.

Occupational schemes

If you are a member of a company pension scheme and still with the company, or

- you left but still have pension rights left with the company scheme (a 'preserved pension')

- you are getting a pension from the scheme

- you are entitled to benefits on the death of someone else who is a member

- you are eligible to join the scheme

you can get a vast amount of information about the scheme, some of it automatically, and some of it if you ask for it. It includes an annual benefit statement, trustees' reports and accounts and who is managing the scheme.

The rules about what you can have and when you can have it are rather complicated; if you have a problem, consult a pensions lawyer or OPAS (see ADDRESSES, page 256) and they can help.

108 Insolvency and bankruptcy

One of the nightmares you might face is that of becoming bankrupt. Among all the other problems you will face, as well as losing reputation, the right to use credit cards and bank accounts, and the loss of a home, the question arises whether you will lose your pension rights as well.

This problem was considered at length by the Goode Committee which looked at pensions reform some years ago; it thought it would be sensible that pension rights were not to be considered part of your estate, to be handed over to creditors on your bankruptcy.

The position is currently in a state of flux and differs whether you have a personal pension or a company pension.

Personal pensions

A case in 1997 seems to state that a personal pension was an asset of the trustee in bankruptcy and would be used to pay creditors, even after you had been discharged from bankruptcy.

This means that if you are under retirement age when you are bankrupt, once you are entitled to the benefits your trustee could require the provider to cash up as much of the pension as possible and hand it over, together with the monthly payments thereafter. The argument is that it was one of your assets when you went bankrupt.

It does seem awfully unfair:

- most occupational pension schemes (see below) give protection against this

- it defeats the objective of discharge which is to enable you to lead your life again

- it goes against the public policy objective which was expressed in the Goode Report which is that pensions built up over the years should be immune from creditors – provided you did not pay the contributions while you were insolvent and deliberately to defeat creditors.

There is a body of pressure building up in the industry to get the law reformed; in any event the law case (*Landau*) which established the precedents may not be of general application. And there are steps you can take to protect your pension (well before bankruptcy is contemplated!).

- Ensure that your personal pension provider has a 'forfeiture clause' or 'protective trust' built into the terms of your scheme; most of the providers have started to do this. It is not certain how effective they are, but they are certainly better than nothing.

- Consider moving (if possible) to an occupational scheme and transferring your personal pension rights over to gain the protection of protective trusts which certainly do work.

Occupational schemes

Your position is much better in an occupational scheme. Almost all schemes contain a clause specifically protecting your pension on bankruptcy. The way it works is that at your bankruptcy your rights are forfeit. The rights go to the trustees who can then either defer payment until you are discharged, or pay someone else, perhaps your spouse. It is very effective and has been tested over many years.

It is not, however, automatic; and a few schemes do not contain such cover, especially statutory schemes (say, police or teachers). This is why the Pensions Act 1995 contained two special sections:

- the first to state categorically that pension rights did not form part of your estate on bankruptcy;

- and second, to specifically allow pension schemes to incorporate in their terms provisions protecting you once the payments have come into operation.

For reasons which are not quite clear, these sections are the only sections of the Pensions Act 1995 that have not been brought into force! But it cannot be too long before they are.

109 Independent financial advisers

Most advisers are now qualified (see page 99), and all are regulated. Most, however, are remunerated (paid) by commission, i.e. by the insurance company or equivalent, rather than by you. This means that however properly the adviser behaves, the advice will always be tainted by the suspicion that it is prompted more by the needs of the insurance company than your own.

It is better, if you can bring yourself to do it, to pay fees for advice. But that can come as something of a shock and you are never quite sure whether the advice you are getting is worth it. There is nothing you can do about finding a reputable and honest adviser; just remember that everyone else is in the same boat, and that advisers, especially if they have been in the game for a while, have a great deal to lose if they make a mess of it.

Remember also that shorter-term contracts are usually better value than long-term contracts (the commission is lower and therefore the charges deducted against your fund are lower). In other words you should normally choose single premium rather than regular or annual premium contracts.

110 Insurance companies

Insurance companies are the (so far) major providers of pensions, although banks and building societies have been permitted to enter the market.

If you are in a company pension scheme of any size, it is likely that your scheme is managed by a scheme manager and staff (either external or internal) rather than by an insurer. In these cases it is called a self-administered scheme.

But almost all personal pensions and very many company schemes are administered and invested by insurance companies.

Some are fine, others are less fine. All are supervised by the government and it is highly unlikely that they will go bust; indeed the big problem is the scale of the reserves they keep which should perhaps be used to improve benefits.

In recent years most of them have received a bit of a knock because of rather foolish and anticipatable problems in selling personal pensions; and in company schemes they have rather too frequently imposed excessive discontinuance charges (surrender penalties). Administration systems have also commonly failed and their overheads have consumed too much, being spent on fancy offices and heavy marketing charges.

None the less the alternatives, such as Virgin and Marks & Spencer, have both improved competition (and made the old household names improve) and given a wider choice, although it is too early to see whether their systems and expenses are any better in the longer term.

__111__ International employees and schemes

Social security

One of the major costs for employers are the social security costs incurred on employment of staff. The UK's is perhaps one of the lowest in Europe, and so it makes sense, if possible, to retain employees in the UK scheme where employees are sent abroad. This is sometimes easiest in the European Union, where there is an extensive multi-lateral system; the advice may be different in other countries.

WHAT IF I AM EMPLOYED IN A NON-EU COUNTRY?

Your employer must pay Class 1 NI contributions on all

earnings paid during the first 52 weeks that you are working abroad, provided

- he has a place of business in the UK, and

- you are ordinarily resident in the UK, and

- you were resident in the UK immediately before starting the employment abroad.

There are definitions of 'place of business' and 'ordinary residence' in the National Insurance rules.

Otherwise there is no liability to pay Class 1 contributions – but you may have the right to pay Class 3 voluntarily, and should normally do so. If you return from time to time, or move overseas for successive periods of employment, there are special rules.

EMPLOYEES IN EU COUNTRIES

If you are employed in a EDU or EEA country, you are normally covered by EU rules, rather than bilateral agreements between the UK and the other countries.

112 Lloyd's underwriters

If you are a Lloyd's underwriter still in business, you are a rather rare bird; you are also still entitled to special (personal) pensions treatment, because of the fact that you cannot find out how much you have earned until at least three years after the year in which you wish to pay pension contributions (and sometimes not even then).

Whether you are a Name or a simple underwriter, you are entitled to use your investment income as 'net relevant earnings', i.e. income on which you can pay pension contributions, and there are special rules allowing you to use earnings from other years on which to calculate how much pension contributions you can make. There were restrictions in relation to years before 1993/4.

113 Lost pensions

If you cannot remember where you put your pension, you could always try getting in touch with the Pensions Registry, who will try to find what happened to your employer many years ago and who is now looking after that scheme.

114 Maternity

If you are pregnant, you are entitled to time off your employment – and to continued membership of your occupational pension scheme. Whether you are entitled to have pensionable service credited while you are off is not yet clear; there is a case in front of the European Court of Justice at the moment. But it is clear that your break is not to be considered a break in service for pension purposes, so you should be protected during your maternity leave.

115 Meetings and minutes

There are strict rules about how pension scheme trustees' meetings are to be conducted. They are not of importance so far as your day-to-day pension affairs are concerned, so they are not set out here; if you would like to learn more, look at some of the books suggested in FURTHER READING (page 258).

116 Members and eligibility

There are strict rules about who can and who cannot be excluded from membership of your company pension scheme. You cannot be excluded on the grounds of sex or race or disability; but you can for the time being be excluded on the grounds of age or because you only work part-time. Some of these discriminations will eventually be outlawed by European Union law.

117 Regulators

See OPRA, PENSIONS OMBUDSMAN, OPAS, CONTRIBUTIONS AGENCY, PENSION SCHEMES OFFICE (Appendices II and III)

118 Retiring

Retirement is very much a twentieth century concept. Until the beginning of the century, unless you were wealthy, you worked until you dropped. Now everyone expects to retire, some as early as 50 or even earlier.

But there is nothing that requires you to retire at any age (unless your contract of employment makes you), although the Employment Rights Act 1996 says that if your employer wants to, he can fire you at State Retirement Age, whatever that may be.

In some cases the State Retirement Age might suit you fine as your retirement age. In other cases you might prefer to retire early (in which case you usually have to settle for a lower pension, because you will be paying in for less time, and drawing out for more).

In other cases, it might suit you to retire later than the formal retirement age. In which case you might be able to draw a larger pension, for just the opposite reasons. In each case there are different rules (of course) depending on whether the pension is a state one, a personal pension or an occupational pension.

State pensions

To get your state pension, you must complete and return a claim form (you will normally be sent one automatically). If it does not come three months before your State Retirement Age (still 65 for men and 60 for women), write to the local Benefits Agency (in the phone book). It is not uncommon for mistakes to happen; there are millions of records of millions of people and even more millions of contributions, and some of them are bound to be wrong, perhaps because your employer filed mistakes several years ago. If it looks all right, it is not easy to challenge it.

A married woman claiming a pension on her husband's contributions must fill in a separate form.

If you deferred your pension at State Retirement Age, to increase the pension later, you must tell the Benefits Agency when you want to start taking it. If you are late claiming your pension, you can only get three months' arrears.

How to receive it

You can choose to get your pension paid:

- by weekly order book, which you need to take to the local post office to cash; your pension is paid one week in advance, and anyone can cash the pension on your behalf (as explained in the order book).

- by direct payment into your bank account (or Girobank, building society or National Savings account) automatically. The money is paid in arrears, and you can choose to take it monthly (four-weekly) or quarterly. If you are also on Income Support, it will be paid weekly in advance together with your Income Support.

Trivial pensions (less than £5 a week) are paid once a year in December in arrears. You normally get the pension paid on the Monday, and you cannot receive pension for days of retirement before the first pay-day. If your spouse receives his or her pension on a different day (usually Thursday), you can elect to have yours on the same day too.

Deferring pensions

You can, if you prefer, defer taking your pension when you get to State Retirement Age; if you do, your pension, when you do take it, will be enhanced.

- Until 2010 the pension is increased by 7.5% a year for each year that you defer it (1/7p in the £ per week); if you defer it for five years, the pension increases by 37.5%. Additional and Graduated Pensions are also increased in the same way. You cannot defer it for more than five years.

- After 2010 the pension will be increased (as above), but by 1/5p per £ per week (or 10.4% p.a.). You can defer for as long as you wish.

Personal pensions

An insurance company or other provider will normally pay your pension net after tax. If you defer it they will usually increase it by a predetermined amount.

Occupational schemes

You will normally get your pension from your company just like you get your salary (only it will be less). The company scheme will deduct PAYE from your pension and forward you the balance, less any amount that has to be paid under an earmarking order to a former spouse (if any).

119 Retirement ages

The idea of a retirement age is a modern notion; until the turn of the century if you needed to work, you worked until you could no longer, perhaps because of ill-health. Now we seem to believe in a retirement age, at which stage in life we are entitled no longer to have to work.

The age, however, differs widely. The State Retirement Age will be equalised at age 65 by 2010, but may eventually (as in Germany and the US) reach 67 or even 70 as the population as a whole ages.

There are also restrictions imposed by the tax authorities on when you can retire from a non-state pension scheme. The normal minimum is 50 and the maximum is 75 (there are separate rules for Retirement Annuity Contracts, the fore-runner to personal pensions); and there are special rules for certain professions (see Table 38).

If you are one of these special people, you are not compelled to take your pension at these ages, it is merely an option not available to other less fortunate people. You can of course defer taking the pension until a later date. (If you change jobs you should run another pension scheme with a different retirement

Table 38 Special retirement ages for certain professions	
Athletes (appearance and prize money only)	35
Badminton players	35
Boxers	35
Cricketers	40
Cyclists (professional)	35
Dancers	35
Divers (saturation, deep sea and free swimming)	40
Downhill skiers	30
Footballers	35
Golfers (tournament earnings)	40
Jockeys (flat racing)	45
Jockeys (National Hunt)	35
Members of the Reserve Forces	45
Models	35
Motorcross motorcycle riders	40
Motorcycle road racing riders	40
Motor racing drivers	40
Real Tennis players	35
Royal Marine Reservists	45
Rugby League players	35
Rugby Union players	35
Speedway riders	40
Squash players	35
Table Tennis players	35
Tennis players	35
Trapeze artists	40
Wrestlers	35

age.) The problem with these seemingly attractive ages is that you still are limited to how much you can put in, like ordinary mortals, and since you have less time to contribute (and less time to roll up the investment income), the benefits you might enjoy will in fact usually be pretty limited.

120 Revaluation

In a company pension scheme the law is that your pension, once in payment, must be index-linked at up to 5%. The pension rights you leave behind in a company scheme, if you move to another company or leave the scheme, must be similarly fully index-linked.

121 Revenue limits

The Inland Revenue impose three kinds of limits on your pension arrangements:

- on the amount you can pay in, which applies mostly to personal pensions

- on the amounts you can build up in a scheme, which applies mostly to company schemes

- and on the amount you can take out (which applies mostly to company schemes).

There are also limits on when you can draw a pension, how much you can contribute by way of additional contributions, how much you can transfer between schemes and many other limits.

These limits are immensely complicated and set out in a series of Inland Revenue Practice Notes which are made available to professional advisers, pension funds and insurance companies. Many of these rules are so complicated that the Revenue themselves find them difficult to administer. In real life it is very difficult without professional advice (and sometimes not even then) to check whether the pension you are thinking of getting is indeed over the maximum or not, and unless the difference between what you expect and what you get is very large, you will normally have to take the calculation on trust.

There is great pressure in the pensions industry to try and simplify the rules, but for the time being, short of using one of the very expensive computer programs which cost around £7,000 p.a., you will not find it possible to cross-check the calculations.

122 Savings

PEPs

PEPs pay no tax on the dividends they receive, and there is no capital gains tax to pay when the shares are sold. Any money held within a PEP is exempt from tax on the interest it earns, so long as the money is used to buy shares later. All tax reclaims are dealt with by the PEP manager (whom you must have). If you put money into a PEP regularly, you can only use one scheme, and the advantage (compared with pensions) is that you can take the money at any time, and there is no tax penalty. There is a wide variety of plans including

- self-select, where you decide how to invest the money and pay a small fee to the manager

- advisory, usually operated by brokers

- managed (discretionary) where the investment decisions are made by the plan manager

- corporate, for investment in shares in one company, usually your employer

- single-company, again limited to investment in one company

- unit trust/investment trust, which spread the risk a little wider, but not all trusts are eligible (they must have at least 50% of their assets in the European Union, including the UK).

The advantages compared with pensions are obvious:

- they are a simple way to provide some form of savings

- they are very tax-efficient (like pensions, although there is no tax relief on the contributions)

- you can use the cash to buy voluntary annuity at retirement – or take tax-free cash at the end

- you can pay management charges on top (there are restrictions in pension arrangements in relation to tax relief on charges)

- the penalties for moving from one manager to another are usually less, much less, than moving from one pensions manager to another

- you can withdraw your dividends tax-free whenever you like

- you can withdraw all or part of your PEP at any time, free of tax.

For retirement purposes, obviously, you would be looking for a PEP that

- decides to go for growth (i.e. increase in the value of the shares) rather than income (i.e. dividends), and that

- uses professional management rather than requiring you to make your own decision as to where the money is invested (unless you have the time and inclination to follow the investments closely), which is normally cheaper for smaller sums, to ensure that there is sufficient spread amongst companies to protect against the risk of one or more investments failing.

Finally the compensation system that applies to company pensions if the investments are stolen or mismanaged does not apply to PEPs; while there is a form of protection through the Personal Investment Authority but it is not as extensive. And it is not certain how long the scheme will be available under the tax rules, whereas pensions seem to have a longer life span.

TESSAs

TESSAs are cash investment accounts offered by banks and building societies just like any other bank account. The money you put in stays in cash; and the scheme has been available since 1991. Both you and your spouse can have a separate TESSA. When interest rates are high enough, i.e. above inflation, they are very attractive, because unless you take the money out before you are supposed to, you pay no tax on it; but if interest rates are low, as they are at the moment (1998) even with the tax break, there may be other things more attractive.

The main restriction is that the money you put in must not

be withdrawn for five years, although the interest can be. If you do, tax is payable. The maximum over the five years you can put in is £9,000 (not more than £3,000 in the first year, not more than £1,800 in each of the following three years and not more than £600 in the final year).

None of this will provide much of a pension, but it can make a useful top-up, and may in certain cases be more attractive than, say, topping up your pension rights.

The other advantage of TESSAs, as compared with topping-up (perhaps by making extra contributions) or other pension arrangements, is that you can take the money (albeit by making some tax) whenever you want; pensions can only be taken as pension and you have to retire.

ISAs

Individual Savings Accounts have been announced by the government but at the time of writing the details are not available. It is likely that they will prove attractive if you have less than, say, £6,000 p.a. to save for your old age; such accounts are likely to prove better value than a personal pension.

123 Survivor's benefits

Normally most company pension arrangements automatically provide survivor's benefits, certainly for married survivors. ('Survivors' is the trendy unisex word for what used to be called widows and widowers.) Personal pensions do not provide these automatically; usually you have to choose whether you want a full pension for yourself, or a reduced pension plus a spouse's pension. And you do not need to tell your spouse before you die which option you have made!

Cohabitees

The problem for cohabitees (i.e. a partner to whom you are not married) is that it is difficult for trustees to find out whether you have been living with the partner for a short time or a long time, and how dependent he or she is.

For a married spouse, it is relatively straightforward for the trustees; with some exceptions, all they have to do is look at the marriage certificate and the death certificate and then pay, say, the widow's pension and any death benefits.

But how can they tell whether your cohabitee is a one-night stand or a love of a lifetime not evidenced by marriage? In such cases they use their discretion to decide whether it is right to pay the money – but that can be a worry for anyone you leave behind, because of the lack of certainty.

Same-sex partners

Similar rules apply to same-sex partners, although it may be that, following a European Court case, equivalent benefits should be provided if they are provided for different sex cohabitees.

The Inland Revenue changed their own rules some years ago to allow trustees, if they wanted, to pay benefits to a same-sex partner even if there was no financial dependency; but it still depends on the feelings and discretion of the trustees. There is no automatic benefit system available.

Widows and widowers

Widows and widowers are now known as 'survivors'; they are dealt with at the beginning of this section.

Dependants

The definition of dependency has been broadened by the Inland Revenue in recent years; it now includes not only financial dependency but also emotional dependency, so that trustees if they wish can also consider people who are dependent on you in a wide range of areas as well as financial.

124 Taxation

The tax structure of pensions works in a very simple way; with some exceptions you get tax relief when you pay the money in, tax relief on the funds you put in, but pay tax on the benefits you receive.

There are some exceptions, however:

- any money that is returned to an employer has 40% tax deducted before it is returned

- if your scheme has too much money in it (sometimes called a surplus), it will have to pay tax on the income on the surplus

- if you cash in some of your pension at retirement, you get the cash tax-free, instead of paying tax on the pension

- the pension fund pays some tax (e.g. VAT, tax on UK dividends, stamp duty).

This tax system, however, is generally regarded as being fiscally neutral (i.e. it avoids double taxation) and recognises that pensions are different from, for example, savings (which, unlike a pension, you can leave to the next generation).

125 Topping-up: how can I improve my pension?

See also CONTRIBUTIONS (page 72)

Most of us have some kind of gap in our career, whether having taken time off to have a family, or suffered a period of unemployment, or having changed jobs which meant a loss of pension rights.

So it is hardly surprising that so many wish to top up the pension arrangements that they do have; in fact only around 1% of the population enjoy the maximum pension permitted under the current Revenue limits. There are several ways in which it is sensible to consider topping up:

- in the state scheme
  - by making additional contributions
  - by making uprated contributions

- by working after retiring
- in your company scheme
- in your personal pension

Each of these is dealt with separately.

Topping up your state pension benefits

If you had a break in your pension record, you can increase your state pension by either (or both)

- making additional contributions to the state scheme and
- deferring taking your benefits to a later date than normal.

MAKING ADDITIONAL CONTRIBUTIONS

You can usually improve your position by making voluntary contributions (called Class 3 contributions) to cover the gap years. You can do this only for gaps within the last six years. Voluntary contributions cannot be paid for years when you were paying contributions at the married woman's reduced rate.

It would be sensible to get a pension forecast (see INFORMATION AND DISCLOSURE, page 216) before making additional contributions; if you have been given Home Responsibilities Protection (i.e. pension credits for time when you spent caring for someone, for example), you already have a full record. But buying extra state pension if you can is usually very sensible; it is very good value for money, index-linked and all the overheads paid for by the state. You would be unlikely to do as well privately.

DEFERRING YOUR PENSION

You can decide not to draw your pension when you get to retirement age, for up to five years after the State Retirement Age. If you have started to take your pension, and then decide to defer it, you can – but you can change your mind only once. A married man whose wife is drawing a pension based on his contributions needs her consent before giving up his pension as she will have to give up hers also.

If you defer your pension, it will be increased by 7.5% a year for each full year that you defer it (around 1/7p in the pound). You have to defer for at least seven weeks to be permitted an increase. A full five-year deferral (the maximum) increases your pension by 37.5%; your other pensions (e.g. Graduated, Additional (SERPS)) are also increased at the same rate. You cannot take one state pension and defer the rest.

If you are a married woman entitled to a pension on your own contributions, and you defer taking it, you will also receive an increase as above. There are some other points.

- If you are a married woman 60–64 who is entitled to a pension only on your husband's contributions, you can defer this as well, to gain an increase. If you are 60+ and your husband defers his pension, you cannot draw the married woman's pension; but once he starts to take his pension, both of you receive increases.

- Your pension based on your husband's contributions will not be increased if, while your husband defers his pension, you take your Additional or Graduated pension.

Some observers think it not sensible to defer taking your pension, arguing that the enhancement for doing so is not actuarially (mathematically) worth it. It would be better, it is said, to take the pension when it is offered (i.e. at State Retirement Age) and if you do not want to spend it, simply leave it in a bank account or invest it. You can at least then leave whatever is left to your heirs. If you leave it with the state, and you die, it is lost and gone for ever. Everyone will have their own opinion on whether it is sensible to defer; a lot will depend on how fit you feel. If you feel you will live for ever, it might be better to go for enhancement. If you are feeling pretty poorly, take the money when it is offered.

Working after retirement

You can take your state pension as soon as you reach State Retirement Age. At one time, if you worked, you lost the pension; this no longer applies and no pension is now reduced by any money you earn in addition (although other benefits may be affected).

You still have to pay tax on both your pension and any earnings – but National Insurance contributions are not deducted (you normally get a certificate of exemption from the Department of Social Security), although the employer still has to pay contributions. You are therefore more attractive to employers who can justify paying you less than younger employees (there is no law against discrimination on the grounds of age).

UPRATING YOUR CONTRIBUTIONS

If you are a woman, you might be paying either no, or reduced-rate, National Insurance contributions. If you are very low paid, perhaps working part-time, earning under around £60 a week, you will pay no NI contributions. If you receive Home Responsibilities Protection (see page 62) you will be building up credits for your Basic Pension. But otherwise you will not, and you will later be invited to make contributions (Class 3) by the DSS to get an improved pension. You will also have a lower earnings record for SERPS (the additional) pension and you might find it more profitable (if you can) to take a proper career break and then work full time, than to work right through and earn lower credits to the Additional Pension.

You should also think about paying full NI contributions so that you can earn a state pension in your own right, not just on the basis on your husband's contributions.

- If you are not married (even if living with a partner), you will not get a widow's pension.

- If you are not married (even if living with a partner), you will not get the married women's pension once he retires after 65.

Age Concern suggests that if you are married and older than him, or less than five years younger, it is worth ensuring that you get some state pension of your own, and that there are other reasons:

- Paying full rate contributions qualifies you for other state benefits (such as Jobseeker's Allowance and Incapacity Benefit) – but you need at least two and a half years' of contributions.

- You get NI credits for periods of sickness.

- You get Home Responsibilities Protection (all other things being equal).

- You can pay extra contributions to fill gaps in your record.

- You might earn Additional Pension, even if you do not qualify for a Basic Pension.

- It might be cheaper! If you are on low earnings, the reduced-rate contributions might actually be higher than the full rate (because the reduced rate is fixed, and the full rate varies depending on the level of earnings).

OTHER SOCIAL SECURITY BENEFITS

If your state pension is low (and you have little in the way of savings or other income), you may be eligible for other social security benefits (Housing Benefit, Income Support, Council Tax Benefit).

Occupational pensions

ADDITIONAL VOLUNTARY CONTRIBUTIONS

Additional Voluntary Contributions (AVCs) are contributions you pay in addition to any contribution you have to pay as a member of your company pension scheme. AVCs provide extra pension benefits (usually) so that you could retire early, for example, or provide additional benefits for your spouse or other dependants on your death. You might not have as much pension as you think you need because you have joined schemes late in life and wish to catch up and improve your own pension. Whatever the reason, AVCs are intended to enable you to make more pension provision than the normal contributions will give you.

AVCs are generally regarded as part of your company pension scheme and are covered by the rules of the scheme (unlike free-standing AVCs; see FSAVCs below). You have a right by law to make AVCs and all company schemes must provide an AVC facility, either by allowing you to make extra payments into the scheme itself and its own investments or through an external agency such as a building society or insurance company. There is a limit to how much you can pay: the maximum you can pay into any company scheme is 15% of your earnings, so that if, for example, your scheme requires you to make a 5% contribution, you can only make another 10% contribution (whether to an AVC or an FSAVC).

If you pay too much (i.e. not more than 15% but even within those limits), you might be buying a pension which will eventually turn out to be more than the Inland Revenue say you can have (broadly, two-thirds of final salary). It is unusual, but can happen if you have been paying for many years, or the scheme is in any event a generous one. It is the job of your scheme administrator to check from time to time whether this is likely to happen (these are called 'headroom checks') so that you can reduce your contributions or even stop them altogether.

If, when you get to retirement age, you find that there is too much money in your pension scheme so that you hit the Inland Revenue limits, you will get the excess back as a lump sum – less some tax, normally at 10%, so it is still a useful thing to do.

When you leave the scheme, you need to stop paying the AVCs (and any FSAVCs) until you join a new scheme. You can then start a new one; normally your AVC fund will remain invested until your pension benefits start or you transfer your arrangements to another scheme. If you transfer your pension arrangements, your AVCs have to follow. And when your benefits are paid at, say, retirement age, you have to use your AVCs at the same time.

If you die before the pension starts, the scheme rules will say what happens to your money. Normally you can tell the trustees beforehand (using something called an 'expression of wish' form) where you would like the money to go; while for tax reasons they are not bound to follow your wishes, they normally will do so.

The benefits you can buy with your AVCs include (subject to the rules of your particular scheme) some or all of:

- a pension payable during your life

- a pension payable for your lifetime together with a pension for your spouse on your death

- a pension payable on your death to your spouse or some other person who was dependent on you (whether financially or otherwise)

- increases on your pension.

Once you have elected how to use your AVCs and, for example, the person dies, you have lost the money; you cannot normally change your decision after the event.

Where you started contributing AVCs before April 1987 you may be able to take some or all of your AVC fund as a tax-free cash sum.

The AVCs' value and security depend on where they are invested (such as the particular building society or insurance company). If your pension scheme is eventually wound up, the AVCs are usually treated with high priority (above other liabilities); and if the scheme was wound up after April 1997 the AVC fund is treated as a separate part of the assets of the pension scheme and has its own priority. Whether the investments have been well-performing depends on the building society or insurer.

It is up to the scheme to decide who looks after your AVCs; it could be the scheme itself, or more usually a building society or insurance company. However, it may be that you would like to decide yourself where the funds are invested, which is why …

FREE-STANDING ADDITIONAL VOLUNTARY CONTRIBUTIONS

… free-standing AVCs were introduced. These allow you to decide where to pay your AVCs, such as an insurance company of your choice. There are some significant differences however between AVCs and FSAVCs, not all in your favour.

- FSAVCs are not part of the pension scheme, although the scheme needs to know about them to do the 'headroom checks' to make sure you are not paying too much in.

- FSAVCs are not therefore part of the supervisory process; they are technically a form of personal pension and therefore regulated by the body that regulates where you have invested, such as an insurance company or unit trust.

- Usually the costs of AVCs (the administration costs) are paid for by your employer as part of the costs of running the scheme; FSAVC costs are paid for by you. So the investments have to perform that much better in order to compete.

- The scheme is not normally permitted under the regulations to advise you whether an AVC or FSAVC is better; you need to take your own independent advice.

- You cannot use any of your FSAVC money to provide lump sum benefits; they can only be used for pension.

SALARY SACRIFICE

An alternative or additional method is to agree to take a lower salary in exchange for extra pension rights; this is known as 'salary sacrifice'. It is crucial that, if this step is taken, it must be carefully documented so that the agreement to take a lower salary does not mention the increased pension contributions and is agreed before the salary reduction takes place. Otherwise the salary sacrifice will not be effective and extra tax will have to be paid. The local inspector will decide whether the sacrifice is effective. In any event the employer is supposed to continue to make a material contribution to the scheme (say, 10% of the total contributions). The benefit of salary sacrifice is that tax and NI are saved on the income foregone while the contributions to the scheme are tax-deductible.

A variation on salary sacrifice is the dividend waiver, under which dividends which would normally be received are given up (before payment). Provided there is no connection between the dividend waiver and the pension payments, the system is accepted.

Alternatively, you could arrange a bonus sacrifice. It is important, however, that the sacrifice is agreed sufficiently long before the year-end (and not during or after the year-end) before the right to it has accrued. If it is retrospective, the scheme does not work. It is up to the local inspector whether he will grant relief.

If it is done properly, dividend waiver or bonus or commission sacrifice is efficient from both National Insurance contributions and income tax viewpoints at a much lower cost to the employee. For example, if you give up commission of £10,000, you only give up £6,000 spendable (after tax at, say, 40%) – and your employer saves just over £1,000 NICs. There is then around £11,000 to spend on pension contributions.

Personal pensions – paying extra contributions

You can also pay extra contributions into a personal pension (i.e. over the annual limits) if you have paid in less than those limits in earlier years. Normally you can use any of the unused reliefs in the last six years.

Paid too much?

It is possible (though usually unlikely) that you have paid into a scheme enough money which would result in benefits at a higher level than the Inland Revenue allow. If that happens, the main scheme benefits are maintained, and the FSAVC provider has to reduce its benefits and return funds to you, less a tax of 34%. It is then treated in a rather complicated way.

- First, you get some money returned to you (out of an overpayment of, say, £1,000 you would get around £660 after tax of 34%).

- The amount you get is regarded as income on which you have paid basic rate tax at 24%, in other words that you have received £868 with no more tax to pay if you only pay basic rate tax.

- You may have to pay more tax, if you are a higher-rate taxpayer, at 16%, in this case another £139. This amounts to a 48% tax altogether.

- Even if you are not a basic rate taxpayer, you cannot recover the tax.

To limit the chances of this happening, the FSAVC provider must build into the calculations the benefits from your scheme (if you pay more than £2,400 p.a. to it). This is called a 'headroom check'. So the chances of a substantial surplus should be slim. There are less complicated rules if you started your FSAVC before April 1987.

126 Trade unions

Trade unions have been surprisingly quiescent in pensions matters in recent years, but they are now showing signs of revived interest. Paradoxically the union movement has found that since the law changed, in that there had to be the opportunity for scheme members to elect trustees of their company scheme, there have actually been fewer union trustees!

There are, however, many helpful guides published by the movement (see 'Further Reading') and the TUC runs a Trade Union Specialists Group to deal with technical matters. Several unions have backed legal action by members attempting to recover losses incurred as a result of leaving company pension schemes and setting up personal pensions when it was inadvisable for them to do so. They also are heavily involved in negotiating in public sector pension arrangements and backing claims by part-timers who feel they have been discriminated against. The union movement also sees itself as having a role to play in the CORPORATE GOVERNANCE (see page 193) argument, and using the assets that pension scheme trustees control to achieve broader ends than merely financial gain. They were particularly grieved that immediately after the election of a Labour government in May 1997 a £5,000m tax was imposed on pension funds, overshadowing by many degrees the cost of VAT on fuel which the previous administration had imposed.

If you are a trade union member, you can use the services of your own union for technical support or join the TUC Member Trustee Network which provides services specifically tailored to the needs of member-nominated trustees; there are around (1997) 800 members on the network and membership is free.

Trade unions are also beginning to offer trustee training following the provisions of the Employment Rights Act 1996 which allows member trustees paid time off for trustee training.

The TUC also backs a Pensioners' Committee to support claims for improvement of benefits for pensioners generally. It also produces a strategy statement which has a number of objectives, including:

- a worry about the decline in state pensions

- the falling number of occupational scheme members, now less than 50% of the workforce

- the fall in value of the Basic State Pension

- the failure of the SERPS system to provide a decent second pension

- the need to make company pension scheme membership compulsory

- the need for employers to make minimum contributions to schemes

- the need to accept that defined contribution schemes also have a part to play in pensions provision

- a need to examine the attraction of industry-wide schemes, which could cover a wider variety of the workforce than company schemes cover. These are particularly attractive to trade unions since the role of unions (as evidenced in Australia, for example) is much greater in such schemes and they could control, for example, the investment policy.

- solve some of the problems posed by company schemes including transfers and transfer of undertakings

- recognition that, for most people, personal pensions incur excess administration and inadequate benefits.

Changes in the workforce may mean that traditional pension provision is no longer appropriate, especially looking at the growth in temporary employment, self-employment, part-time employment, second-job holders, flexibility and insecurity of even conventional employees. A working group is looking at alternative methods.

Collective bargaining

Trade unions still play a modest part in negotiating on pension rights, but in order to do so freely need to distance themselves from trusteeship, so that few unions now wish to be represented on the boards of trustees.

It is important to distinguish between negotiating on pension rights with the employer and discussing improvement of pension benefits with the trustees, who have no employment relationship with you and your colleagues. A guide to collective bargaining is mentioned in 'Further Reading'.

Trusteeship

At one time trade unions sought automatic representation on trustee boards; such requirements no longer appear, but there is no objection to seeking to elect a trade union representative as a member-elected trustee, although, because of the potential liabilities, few wish to do so.

127 Transfers

You are increasingly rare if you are the kind of person who spends his entire career without changing jobs or employment status (e.g. employed, self-employed, unemployed, carer). Most of us have complex lives, and on average most of us change jobs around four times during our working lives.

Since pensions are related (until the rules change) with employment, the pensions change also. You might want to move your pension rights from one employer to another, or from one personal pension provider to another, or from a personal pension to a company scheme or the reverse.

Making a transfer, however, can be complicated:

- the tax reliefs differ in personal pensions and in company schemes; the Revenue impose controls on moving from one to the other

- the benefits and contributions differ in many schemes; some are based on limiting contributions, others on limiting benefits

- the way in which transfer values are calculated depends on a variety of circumstances; usually (see below) they are not in your favour.

Transferring your pension to another scheme

If you have left your job, you are probably entitled to a 'preserved pension' from your previous scheme, that is, a pension that is kept on ice until you get to retirement age. You could either:

- leave your rights with the old scheme, or

- transfer your rights to your new employer's scheme, or

- transfer your rights to a personal pension.

Deciding whether to transfer or not is a tricky decision to make and it is usually best to take advice from an independent financial adviser. Unfortunately advisers have to complete so much paperwork these days (because they used to give the advice that gave them the most commission in the past) that very few feel able to give the time to give advice. In practice, you will find that in most cases it is best to leave your pension rights where they were.

You do however have a right to transfer your pension from a company scheme to another pension arrangement if you left your previous company's pension scheme after January 1986 (a previous limit) and you are not within one year of that scheme's normal retirement age. You might still be able to transfer your rights even if you left before 1986, but you are unlikely to have the right to insist; it depends on the scheme rules.

You can get a statement of the pension you left behind and its transfer value (how much you can transfer to a new scheme) at least once a year without charge. You may need to ask for this in writing, and the scheme has to let you know within two months of your request.

Once you have the statement you can decide whether it is better to leave it there or move it. It is often best, if you can, to discuss whether to move it with the scheme manager of your new scheme (if possible). If you do decide to move it, you again have to write (usually on a special form sent to you by your old scheme) to give them authority to transfer it. They normally do it within a month; if it takes longer than six months, they have to pay interest on it, and they must pay within twelve months in any event. They will not usually accept instructions from either your new scheme or your financial adviser; they need them from you personally.

However, your new scheme has an option as to whether or not to accept a transfer payment from your old scheme. Sometimes they will not, especially if there might be a need to meet the costs of equal treatment (if the old scheme cannot give a guarantee about any hidden equal treatment liabilities, for example). You might then have to leave it where it is, or transfer to a personal pension.

You are, as mentioned, entitled to a quotation as to the value of the transfer. That quotation is usually guaranteed for a period of time, but if you delay accepting the transfer after that time it is possible the value will change. Values change normally because of changes in interest rates, or tax rates, or annuity rates in the market.

The transfer could be delayed (almost certainly will be) if the former employer has gone out of business or the scheme is being closed down, because (see CLOSURE OF MY SCHEME, page 113) it could take a few years to close the scheme down and pay everyone out. In such a case the transfer value could be reduced or even increased.

If the scheme has a deficit, it is possible that the transfer value will be reduced. In such a case it might be sensible to leave the fund where it is until the deficit is made up some time in the future, if you think that is likely. Alternatively you could take the reduced transfer value and cut your losses.

Errors do occur from time to time in the calculation of transfer values and it is possible to ask the scheme to review them and to check, for example, whether the pensionable pay on which the calculations are performed was correct, or a transfer from a previous scheme was included.

Transfer values do not represent a fund of money – or even your contributions. They reflect the value of a promise to pay benefits, and the value of that promise can fluctuate according to the values of the underlying assets or the cost of annuities. Values are affected by investment conditions and interest rates, for example. If interest rates fall, the amount the fund could buy by way of pension also falls, so that the cost rises – as does a transfer value. And if interest rates rise, the transfer value falls.

What happens when you transfer to a new scheme

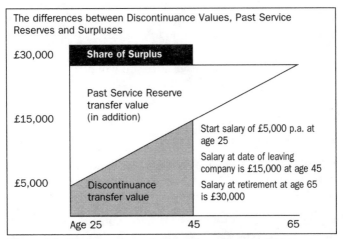

The differences between Discontinuance Values, Past Service Reserves and Surpluses

£30,000 — Share of Surplus

Past Service Reserve transfer value (in addition)

£15,000

Start salary of £5,000 p.a. at age 25

Salary at date of leaving company is £15,000 at age 45

£5,000 — Discontinuance transfer value

Salary at retirement at age 65 is £30,000

Age 25   45   65

Figure 16 What happens when you transfer your rights

Transfer values in a money-purchase scheme are relatively straightforward; it is usually the value of your fund (less any charges or penalties). But the transfer value in your 'final salary' scheme may or may not buy you equivalent years of service in your new employer's fund, for reasons that are explained in Figure 16.

In cases where you have transferred to a personal pension and think you were inadvised to do so (because it would have been better value to stay in the scheme), you have the right to have the transfer examined by your adviser and reviewed. It is likely that if you were persuaded out of a company scheme, you will be entitled to compensation or reinstatement into the former scheme (if they will have you). Complaints should be made to your adviser, provider (insurer) or the Personal Investment Authority Ombudsman.

From April 1997 you are entitled to the legal right to a transfer value whenever you left your scheme (even if it was before 1 January 1986), provided your scheme is not a public service scheme (such as for policemen, firemen, teachers or local authority employees). You are also entitled to a written statement of a guaranteed transfer value; if you accept within three months you will get the figure in the statement.

128 Widows and widowers ('survivors')

State benefits

Widows

You will need to consider whether you will get:

- a Basic State Pension

- some additional pension

- a Widow's Payment (cash sum)

- a Widowed Mother's Allowance

- a private pension.

If you are under 60 when your husband dies, you will get (normally) a state Widow's Pension. Once you reach 60 you can decide whether

- to continue to receive it for another five years, or

- to take the Retirement Pension.

You will also get a lump sum Widow's Payment (£1,000) if you are under 60 when he dies, or over 60 and he either was under 65 or had deferred taking his State Pension.

If you are 55–64 when your husband dies (and you have not started to receive a State Retirement Pension), you will normally receive a Widow's Pension of £64.70 (taxable) (you will get less if your husband's record is not a full one unless he died because of an industrial accident or disease).

You also get an Additional Pension based on your husband's earnings, either from the State (if your husband was contracted-in) or from the company or personal pension scheme (if contracted-out).

If you are between 45 and 55 when your husband dies, you will probably get a reduced age-related pension, 7% lower for each year that you are younger than 55. At 45 you will only get around 30% of the full rate. Your pension will not increase as you get older (although it will be index-linked).

Widowed Mother's Allowance

Whatever age you were when your husband died, if you have children you will receive a widowed mother's allowance until they reach 16 (or 19 if still in full-time education). When they stop being dependent, you can move on to receiving a widow's pension.

After you get to 60

After you reach the State Retirement Age (still 60) you can then take the Basic State Pension, based on your own or your husband's contributions, if this gives a better pension. And if you are over 60 when your husband dies and not receiving a full Basic Pension, you can use his record to get a full pension.

And, if you are both over State Pension Age (60 for you and 65 for him) when he dies, you will also get his Additional Pension (as well as any you have) up to the level of the maximum Additional Pension for a single person (less any amount for the time you and your husband were contracted out of SERPS). If he dies after April 2000, you can get only half his Additional Pension.

For what it's worth, you will also get half your husband's Graduated Pension as well as any based on your own contributions.

The widow's option

If you are a widow you can choose between

- taking the Widow's Pension until you are 65 (rather than stop at 60), or

- stop taking the Widow's Pension and take the Retirement Pension (plus whatever Graduated Pension there is).

If your husband's company scheme was contracted-out you will get a Widow's Guaranteed Minimum Pension (or Protected Right's Widow's Pension) on his death, and this does not stop when you get to pension age; and if you have a pension from your own company pension scheme, you should be able to take a pension from that at 60 without it being reduced by the value of the Widow's Pension.

Widowers

Widowers get a rough deal in pensions; all the sympathy and the money is with widows. All you get (if you lost your wife after April 1979), and you do not have a good enough contributions record of your own, is:

- a Basic Pension based on your wife's contributions – provided you were both over pension age when she died

- half your wife's Graduated Pension (tiny)

- her Additional Pension (only half after April 2000) plus your own, up to the maximum Additional Pension for a single person.

But if you lose your wife before you make it to 65, there is no widower's pension; when you get to retirement age, you can use your wife's contribution record instead of your own if this improves the pension.

129 Women

By and large women as a group have inferior pensions to those of men. Not only do they earn less (and have proportionately lower pensions) but many are part-time workers and hence frequently have not historically been eligible to become a member of a company scheme, or have enough disposable income to pay contributions to a personal pension.

Only about 28% of women receive a full state pension in their own right, and 37% of women receive under £40 a week. From 2020 the retirement age will be 65 for women (like men) by which time the joint retirement age is likely to be even higher, perhaps 70. So, pension entitlements will be less than those for the present generation; in normal times if receipt of pension is deferred from 60 to 65, the retirement pension would increase by 37.5%. Not only, therefore, is the retirement age increasing, but the increase will disappear.

Whether there will be any improvement in the situation for women is doubtful. A recent survey suggested that:

- many women do not receive a pension from the state in their own right, despite having worked in paid employment for many years, were not acquainted with their husband's pension entitlements (despite the fact that they rely on it for their source of income) nor do they know what they would be entitled to were they to survive their husbands

- the level of the state pension is inadequate and becoming worse, yet many women have and will have no other source of income in their old age, and the difference between men's and women's income is increasing

- many women have never had the opportunity to make adequate provision for retirement; there is a recommendation (which finds echoes in other similar reports) that such individuals ought to have contributions paid for them by the state into a private retirement account

- the present system assumes women's reliance on men, which is no longer a valid assumption

- pensions are too complicated for women; this rather politically incorrect conclusion is accepted in the case of men too in many other studies.

Whether indeed women need special treatment in pension arrangements is an argument that will no doubt continue for years to come. It is however correct to conclude that most pension systems reflect a male pattern of lifetime employment, and redesigning a system to cope with new social patterns will take some time and will not be easy.

SECTION

G

Appendices

▌ Abbreviations

ACT	Advance Corporation Tax
AVC	Additional Voluntary Contributions
CBI	Confederation of British Industry
CETV	Cash Equivalent Transfer Value
CGT	Capital Gains Tax
EEA	European Economic Area
EMU	European Monetary Union
FSA	Financial Services Act
FSAVC	Free-standing Additional Voluntary Contributions
FURBS	Funded Unapproved Retirement Benefits Scheme
GPP	Group Personal Pensions
HRP	Home Responsibilities Protection
IFA	Independent Financial Adviser
ISA	Individual Savings Account
LEL	Lower Earnings Limit
LPI	Limited Price Indexation
MFR	Minimum Funding Requirement
NAPF	National Association of Pension Funds
OPAS	Occupational Pensions Advisory Service
OPDU	Occupational Pensions Defence Union
OPRA	Occupational Pensions Regulatory Authority
PCB	Pensions Compensation Board
PEP	Personal Equity Plan
PIA	Personal Investment Authority
PRAS	Pension Relief at Source
RAC	Retirement Annuity Contract
RPI	Retail Prices Index
SERPS	State Earnings-related Pensions

SIPP	Self-invested Personal Pension
SSAS	Small Self-administered Pension Scheme
TESSA	Tax Exempt Special Savings Account
UEL	Upper Earnings Limit
UURBS	Unfunded Unapproved Retirement Benefits Scheme

▋▋ Addresses and associations

Actuaries

The Association of Consulting Actuaries (1 Wardrobe Place, London EC4V 5AH) provide a useful list of consulting actuaries; handy for establishing SSASs.

The professional body is the Institute of Actuaries (in Scotland, the Faculty), but they do not generally deal with the public unless there is a complaint about an actuary's service. (Institute of Actuaries, Staple Inn Hall, High Holborn, London WC1V 7QJ; 0171 242 0106; and Faculty of Actuaries, 17 Thistle Street, Edinburgh EH2 1DF; 0131 220 4555.)

Advice

See ACTUARIES AND THEIR REPORTS (page 107) and INDEPENDENT FINANCIAL ADVISERS (page 220)

Compensation

Pensions Compensation Board (Room 501, 5th Floor, 11 Belgrave Road, London SW1V 1RB; 0171 828 9794, fax 0171 931 7239) pays out where there is a deficit in an occupational scheme, there has been dishonesty and the employer cannot make good the deficit.

Disputes and complaints

COMPANY SCHEMES

Occupational Pensions Advisory Service, 11 Belgrave Road, London SW1V 1RB (0171 233 8080).

Pensions Ombudsman, 11 Belgrave Road, London SW1V 1RB (0171 834 9144).

Occupational Pensions Regulatory Authority, Invicta House, Trafalgar Place, Brighton, East Sussex BN1 4BY (01273 627600, fax 01273 627630).

PERSONAL PENSIONS

Personal Investment Authority, 1 Canada Square, Canary Wharf, London E14 5AZ (0171 538 8860).

Personal Investment Authority Ombudsman, 1 Canada Square, Canary Wharf, London E14 5AZ; 0171 538 8860 (to be merged into one body with all the others called Financial Services Authority).

Insurance Ombudsman (135 Park Street, London SE1 9EA; 0171 928 7600) can look at personal and group pensions operated by insurance companies, but you would probably be better off with the Pensions Ombudsman or PIA Ombudsmen.

INVESTMENT MANAGEMENT

Investment Managers Regulatory Organisation, Lloyds Chambers, 1 Portsoken Street, London E1 8BT; 0171 390 5000 (to be merged into one body with all the others called Financial Services Authority).

FINANCIAL ADVICE

Personal Investment Authority, 1 Canada Square, Canary Wharf, London E14 5AZ; 0171 538 8860 (to be merged into one body with all the others called Financial Services Authority).

Financial advisers

A list of financial advisers in your area who charge fees rather than commission (qualified, but not necessarily recommended) is available from the Money Management Register of Fee Based Advisers, Matrix Data Ltd, Freepost 22 (SW1565), London W1E 7EZ, provided you send them your address and postcode.

IFA Promotions can also give you three members in your area if you phone 0171 971 1177.

Lists are available from The Society of Financial Advisers, 20 Aldermanbury, London EC2V 7HY (0171 417 4419) and The Institute of Financial Planning, Whitefriars Centre, Lewins Mead, Bristol BS1 2NT (0117 930 4434) but they cannot tell you who is suitable for you.

Some chartered accountants provide financial advice. The Institute of Chartered Accountants in England and Wales, Moorgate Place, London EC2P 2BJ (0171 920 8711); or, in Scotland, the Institute of Chartered Accountants in Scotland, 27 Queen Street, Edinburgh EH2 1LA (0131 225 5673).

Solicitors are increasingly providing advice: The Law Society, 113 Chancery Lane, London WC2A 1PL (0171 242 1222); in Scotland, the Law Society of Scotland, 26 Drumsheugh Gardens, Edinburgh EH3 7YR (0131 226 7411); and especially the highly efficient Solicitors for Independent Financial Advice (SIFA), 01372 721172.

Investment management

The Association of Private Client Investment Managers and Stockbrokers, 112 Middlesex Street, London E1 7HY provides a list of members.

Solicitors operate the Association of Solicitor Investment Managers (ASIM), Chiddingstone Causeway, Tonbridge, Kent TN11 8JX (01892 870065).

Legal advice

With all the free advice available from the internal dispute resolution arrangements, or from the Occupational Pensions Advisory Service, you should not normally need much legal advice; but if you do, you are better off with a specialist pensions lawyer rather than a High Street lawyer. You can get a list from the Association of Pension Lawyers, 29 Ludgate Hill, London EC4 7JQ (0171 329 6699).

Lost pensions

Pension Schemes Registry, PO Box 1NN, Newcastle upon Tyne NE99 1NN (0191 225 6393) where you have changed jobs in the past or a former employer has been taken over, and you may have money in pension schemes that you have lost touch with. The Registry may be able to help you trace the scheme and so enable you to pursue your rights.

Overseas and abroad

Department of Social Security, Pensions and Overseas Benefits Directorate (Payments), Tyneview Park, Whitley Road, Benton, Newcastle upon Tyne NE98 1BA (0191 218 7777).

The International Employee Benefits Association organises seminars and professional examinations for those specialising in international aspects of employee benefits (including pensions): IEBA, c/o Ms Bernadette Wilkins, Towers Perrin, Castlewood House, 77–91 New Oxford Street, London WC1A 1PX.

Pressure groups

Help the Aged, St James Walk, Clerkenwell Green, London EC1R OBE (0171 253 0253).

War pensions

The War Pensions Agency, Norcross, Blackpool FY4 3WP (01253 858858).

▌▌▌ Further reading

Bankruptcy and liquidation

There are many learned articles on what happens to your pension if you become bankrupt; they are mostly academic.

If your company goes bust, the OPAS guide *Winding-up of Pension Schemes on Company Insolvency: A Guide for Trustees* is a useful, practical guide, though a little dated now. It also publishes a leaflet for scheme members, *Winding-up a Pension Scheme*, also free.

Bluffers guides

Pensions Terminology (with 177 new definitions since the Pensions Act 1995!), Pensions Management Institute (0171 247 1452).

Complaints

Pensions Ombudsman, *The Pensions Ombudsman – What He Can Do ...*, Pensions Ombudsman, free (0171 834 9144).

Pensions Ombudsman, *Annual Report*, free, availability as above.

Office of the Pensions Ombudsman, *Digest of Cases Determined in the Year 1996–97*, free, as above.

Contracting-out

Contracting-out is normally a matter for the employer, not for you. If you must look at the literature, there is a series of DSS manuals: CA14 and CA14A *Termination of Contracted-out Employment* (November 1996), CA14B *Contracted-out Guidance on Re-elections for Salary-related Pension Schemes* (November 1996), CA14C *Contracted-out Guidance for Salary-related Schemes* (November 1996), CA14D *Contracted-out Guidance for Money-purchase Pension Schemes* (November 1996) and CA14E

Contracted-out Guidance for Mixed Benefit Pension Schemes (January 1997), C14F *Technical Guidance on Review of Determinations*, CA15 *Cessation of Contracted-out Pension Schemes*, and C16 *Appropriate Personal Pension Scheme Manual* (all free).

Contributions

The press are full of articles about making additional contributions; a simple leaflet is OPAS, *What are AVCs?*, free from OPAS.

Disabled

First port of call is *Incapacity Benefit: Information for New Customers* (free from Benefits Agency, IB 202, October 1996). Also handy for company scheme benefits is OPAS, *Ill-health Early Retirement*, free from OPAS.

Disputes

A research study of some incomprehensibility is Dundon-Smith and others, *Pension Scheme Inquiries and Disputes*, Social Security Research Report No. 66, Stationery Office, 1997. A more practical guide (more for the professional adviser than the consumer) is Robin Ellison, *Pensions Disputes, Law Practice and Alternatives*, Sweet and Maxwell, 1995. Also useful is OPAS, *Pension Problems, a Review of OPAS Cases 1996/97*, free from OPAS.

Employers

Oddly, there are relatively few resources available to employers trying to make sense of the plethora of options; normally they have to rely on advisers of one sort or another. In giving advice it might be useful to read through *A Guide to the Financial Services Act for Employers*, which sets out what employers can and cannot do when selling their scheme to employees (DSS, leaflet PP4, October 1994, phone 0345 313233).

Europe

To look at how Europe has changed and affected UK pension provision, a study by Linda Luckhaus and Graham Moffat, *Serving the Market and People's Needs: The Impact of European Union Law on Pensions in the UK*, Joseph Rowntree Foundation, 1996.

Information

Registrar of Pension Schemes, Occupational Pensions Regulatory Authority, PO Box 1NN, Newcastle Upon Tyne NE99 1NN (0191 225 6394).

BA Storage and Distribution Centre, Manchester Road, Heywood, Lancashire OL10 2PZ supplies leaflets from the Benefits Agency if you have a problem with local offices or post offices; or if it's just leaflets on pensions, try the very helpful Pensions Info-Line on 0345 31 32 33 (DSS Pensions, FREEPOST BS5555/1, Bristol BS99 1BL).

Customer Services Unit, Pensions and Overseas Benefits Directorate, Room TD015, Tyneview Park, Whitley Road, Benton, Newcastle upon Tyne NE98 1BA (0191 218 7878, fax 0191 218 7293) supplies a range of very useful leaflets on overseas pensions arrangements.

A short leaflet is OPAS, *Getting Information about Your Pension*, free from OPAS. Also useful is OPAS, *Where is My Pension?*, a short leaflet available by post or from a Citizens' Advice Bureau.

Legal texts

For the Full Monty, including all the technical legal information, Robin Ellison (ed.) *The Pensions Practice*, Pendragon (0800 289520).

Magazines

COMPANY SCHEMES

The pensions arena publishes more than the market can truly bear. The industry standard monthly and useful reading if you are going to be a trustee of a company scheme is *Pensions World* (Tolleys, 0181 686 9141). *Pensions Management* is designed more for brokers (FT magazines, 0171 405 6969) and is more trade-oriented.

More readable (again, for company schemes) is *Occupational Pensions* (0171 354 5858) which is designed for scheme managers, but is beautifully produced.

PERSONAL PENSIONS

If you have a personal pension, *Money Management* (0171 405 6969) is expensive but contains frequent comparative surveys of performance (depressing, very often). *Planned Savings* is also useful.

Moving schemes

A simple leaflet is OPAS, *Where is my pension?* (0171 233 8080).

Personal pensions

For the latest figures and who is doing best and worst amongst the pension providers, see the monthly tables in *Money Management* and *Planned Savings*. There are two comprehensive studies which are annual guides; the latest at the time of writing are Janet Walford, *FT Personal Pensions 1998*, 11th edn, Pearson Professional, and John Sheffield, *FT Executives' and Directors' and Top-up Pensions*, 2nd edn, Pearson Professional, which contain probably more than you want to know about pensions.

A simple guide is *Personal Pensions for the Self-employed* (DSS PP3, April 1997) and *Personal Pensions – A Guide for Tax* (Inland Revenue, IR 78).

If you have a problem about a personal pension, see OPAS, *Personal Pension Problems? Where to go for help*, free from OPAS.

Reform

Pension Provision Group (DSS), *We All Need Pensions – The Prospects for Pension Provision*, Stationery Office, June 1998 ('The Ross Report') sets out the prospects for reform with the introduction of 'stakeholder' pensions in mind, the pensions that are likely to replace the basic state and SERPS pension. Lots of facts and figures and robust common sense.

Research and development

Pensions Research Accountants Group c/o GAAPS Ltd, Grafton House, 2–3 Golden Square, London W1R 3AD (0171 437 8899) is a somewhat esoteric organisation dedicated to looking at abstruse technicalities of administration and accounting. Unlikely to be of interest to most consumers.

Retiring

There is no shortage of books on what to do when retiring. Free (and good) from the DSS Benefits Agency is *Retiring? Your Pension and Other Benefits* (FB6, April 1997) and *Benefits after Retirement: What You Could Claim as a Pensioner* (Benefits Agency, FB32, August 1995).

SERPS and Contracting-out

Contracted-out Employments Group, Department of Social Security, Contributions Agency, Newcastle upon Tyne NE98 1YX.

State benefits

There are lots of useful, readable booklets published by government departments (many of which have been used in the preparation of this book). A simple guide to the changes coming in to the state pension is *Changes to Your Future: Will the Pensions Act Affect your State Pension?* (Benefits Agency, EQP 201, February 1996). For changes to the State Retirement Age, i.e. raising it for women, see Department of Social Security, *Equality in State Pension Age: A Summary of the Changes* (EQP1a, February 1996).

The Benefits Agency also publishes *Retiring? Your Pension and Other Benefits* (FB6, April 1997) as well as *Benefits after Retirement: What You Could Claim as a Pensioner* (FB32, August 1995) and *Which Benefit: A Guide to Social Security and NHS Benefits* (FB2, October 1996). Incapacity benefit is dealt with by *Incapacity Benefit: Information for New Customers* (IB 202, October 1996) and the most recent rates of benefit are set out every year in *Social Security Benefit Rates* (NI196, usually every January). Also useful might be *National Insurance Contributions for Married Women* (CA13, October 1996). These leaflets are available from the Pensions Info-Line on 0345 31 32 34 (DSS Pensions, FREEPOST BS5555/1, Bristol BS99 1BL).

Two comprehensive guides if you are going overseas are *National Insurance Abroad* (NI 132, August 1995) designed for employers but also useful for employees, and *Social Security Abroad* (NI 38, April 1997) as well as guides on selected individual countries; look also at *Pensioners or Widows Going Abroad* (NI 106, April 1994) and *Your Social Security Insurance, Benefits and Health Care Rights in the European Community* (SA 29, October 1996).

Statistics

Jonquil Lowe, *Pensions: A Way Forward*, Government Actuary's Department, 1997.

Government Statistical Service, *Social Trends* 27, Office of National Statistics.

Trade bodies

Association of Consulting Actuaries, 1 Wardrobe Place, London EC4V 5AH (0171 248 3163) is a trade association of consulting rather than insurance actuaries. They produce a range of useful literature about what actuaries do – and will find one for you if you need one.

Association of Pension Lawyers, 29 Ludgate Hill, London EC4 7JQ (0171 329 6699); a group of lawyers who talk about pensions. They don't produce things to read (apart from an excellent technical newsletter) but you can get the name of a local pensions lawyer from them.

Faculty of Actuaries, 17 Thistle Street, Edinburgh EH2 1DF (0131 220 4555); the association for Scottish Actuaries which works closely with the English association (Institute of Actuaries).

Institute of Actuaries, Staple Inn Hall, High Holborn, London WC1V 7QJ (0171 242 0106); the professional association of actuaries, conducts examinations and imposes professional discipline on actuaries. If you are not happy about an actuary you use, complain to them.

National Association of Pension Funds, 12–18 Grosvenor Gardens, London SW1W 0DH (0171 730 0585); an association of company 'final salary' and money-purchase pension funds (including local authority pension schemes). Produces a stream of useful publications, including an annual survey of what company schemes are doing, policy documents, and leaflets and guides designed for the public, almost all of which are free.

Pensions Management Institute, 4–10 Artillery Lane, London E1 7LS (0171 247 1452) is the professional body for pension fund managers, and operates the training and examination system for the industry.

Society of Pension Consultants, St Bartholomew House, 92 Fleet Street, London EC4Y 1DH (0171 353 1688); does what it says on the can. Produces a very useful monthly summary of changes but for technicians rather than the public.

Trade unions

TUC, *The Future for Pensions* (1997) sets out an agenda
for reform along union lines; the TUC also publishes *The
1995 Pensions Act – a TUC Guide* (1997) as well as *Model
Statement of Investment Principles, Model Internal
Disputes Procedures and Pensions Act Checklist for
Member Nominated Trustees*, all 1997. The TUC publishes
a quarterly *Pensions Briefing* and has delivered a series of
studies of the personal pensions selling fiasco called *Still No
Justice* (December 1996) and *Justice Delayed*. In relation to
corporate governance, the TUC issues *TUC Shareholder
Voting Guidelines* and a guide for pensions negotiators
Getting the Best from Defined Contribution Schemes (July
1997). This is a companion volume to the TUC Handbook
on *Occupational Pensions for Negotiators and Trustees*.
Also designed for trustees is a periodical *TUC Member
Trustee News* and it has developed a computer-based
training course *Computer-based Training Course for
Member-trustees*.

Transfers

Deciding whether to move pension rights elsewhere is often
a problem; OPAS publish *Transferring a Pension to
Another Scheme*, free.

Trustee

If you decide to agree to be a trustee, you might find it
helpful to have a book by your side, and attend a training
course. Lists of training courses are set out in most of the
pensions magazines. Books include: Robin Ellison, *The
Pensions Trustees Handbook*, 2nd edn 1997, Thorogood
(0171 824 8257).

Roger Self, *Tolley's Pension Fund Trustee Handbook*, 4th edn,
August 1998, £22, ISBN 1–86012 789–X.

Clark Whitehill publish a useful checklist, *A Trustees's
Guide to the Pensions Act 1995* (March 1997, 0171 353
1577, free) which sets out some of the compliance duties.

Very comprehensive, but don't panic at the size of the job; you are certainly complying without realising it.

You would also find it useful, if you are a trustee, to find a copy of the application pack for the Occupational Pensions Defence Union, with a leaflet called *New Defence Union* which explains some of the problems of being a trustee, and what to do about them.

Widows (see also Women)

The fullest guide is *Widows' Benefits* (Benefits Agency, NP 45 from April 1996).

Women

There is an embarrassment of books about women and pensions. The DSS publish three useful guides: *Married Women – An Introduction to the State Retirement Pension* (Benefits Agency, WRP 1, November 1994), *Divorced Women – An Introduction to the State Retirement Pension* (Benefits Agency, WRP 2, November 1994) and *Widowhood – An Introduction to the State Retirement Pension* (Benefits Agency, WRTP 3, November 1994).

If you are interested in pensions policy and women, you might try, amongst a large volume of material, Help the Aged, *Women and Pensions, a Discussion Paper*, 1997.

IV Information about your pension

Information entitlements

You are entitled to a wide range of information about your scheme, including copies of the trust deeds, and in particular to a personal benefit statement, a trustees' report and a member's booklet about the scheme generally.

PERSONAL BENEFIT STATEMENT

The contents of the statement depend on what kind of

Table 39 When you are entitled to a benefit statement

Defined benefit scheme ('final salary' scheme)	Only on request, but within two months; you can make a further request after a year
Defined contribution (money-purchase) scheme	Provided automatically once a year to all current and deferred members
Benefits from a contracted-out scheme based on protected rights	Provided automatically once a year to all current and deferred members
Former members with deferred benefits	Provided automatically once a year to all current and deferred members and the statement must show your date of withdrawal from the scheme.

Table 40 Information you are entitled to on your statement

Defined benefit schemes

- Pension at normal retirement date or date of withdrawal
- Survivor's benefits on death in retirement
- Death-in-service benefits
- Date of entry to pensionable service
- Accrual rate or formula to calculate benefits
- Final pensionable salary
- Details of any deductions from benefits

Defined contribution schemes (including defined contribution AVCs)

- Contributions paid in the immediately preceding scheme year
- The value of the member's account at the date of the statement
- The transfer value at the date of the statement (if different from the value of the account)

Contracted-out (protected rights basis)

- Employer's minimum contributions paid during the immediately preceding scheme year
- Age-related rebates credited during the immediately preceding scheme year
- Date of birth (used to verify age-related rebate)
- Name and address of contact for any correction to date of birth
- Value of the member's Protected Rights Account at the date of the statement
- Transfer value at the date of the statement (if different from the value of the account)

Note Values for Protected Rights Accounts can be given at a different date from the date applicable for other benefits. So, for example, the Protected Rights Account value may be given at 5 April even if the scheme anniversary date is different.

Source: Gissings

scheme you have, and what are the benefits provided under it; and there is no requirement to identify separately defined benefits (e.g. added years) arising from AVCs though this is normally done.

Table 41 What you are entitled to in your members' booklet

Eligibility

- Who is eligible to be a member
- Is entry subject to the member applying, or automatic
- The conditions for eligibility, e.g. age, length of service
- The period of notice required to terminate membership
- Whether re-entry is possible and on what terms

Contributions

- How members' normal contributions are calculated
- How the employer's contributions are calculated
- The arrangements for the paying of AVCs

Benefits

- Normal pension age
- Definition of pensionable earnings
- Rate of benefit accrual
- The benefits payable and how they are calculated
- Payment conditions for scheme benefits, including survivor's benefits, e.g. whether spouse's pension ceases on remarriage

Pension increases

- Details of pension increases and whether they are discretionary
- Where there is the possibility of discretionary increases, who has this power

Source: Gissings

Table 42 Contribution rates for personal pensions 1998/9

Maximum		
Age	% net relevant earnings	Amount
Up to 35	17.5	£15,330
36–45	20	£17,520
46–50	25	£21,900
51–55	30	£26,280
56–60	35	£30,660
61–74	40	£35,040

V   What about the future?

There is no shortage of plans to change the system. Set out below are just some of the bright ideas around in the last few years. Very few of them stand an earthly of being brought in, but they all influence in some way the trend towards privatisation of the state scheme and funding of the system – and improved simplification.

Association of British Insurers, *Pensions: A Long Term Strategy*, June 1997 mimeo.

National Association of Pension Funds, *Securing the Future – Evidence to the Retirement Income Inquiry*, 1996

Sir John Anson (Chairman), *The Retirement Income Inquiry: Pensions 2000 and beyond*, 1996

Maria Evandrou, *Baby Boomers: Ageing in the 21st Century*, Age Concern, 1997.

Deborah Roseveare, Willi Leibfritz, Douuglas Fore and Eckhard Wurze, *Ageing Populations, Pensions Systems and Government Budget Simulations for 20 OECD Countries*, OECD, Paris 1996.

Consumers' Association policy report: A Blueprint for Better Pensions, Consumers' Association, 1997 (0171 830 6000).

Notes

Index

Notes